Learning to Change:
An LEA School-focused Initiative

Dedication

We dedicate this volume to the teachers of Sheffield with whom we have learnt so much.

Learning to Change:
An LEA School-focused Initiative

Edited by

Elizabeth Clough, Kath Aspinwall and
Bob Gibbs

 The Falmer Press
(A member of the Taylor & Francis Group)
London, New York and Philadelphia.

UK   The Falmer Press, Rankine Road, Basingstoke, Hampshire, RG24 0PR

USA   The Falmer Press, Taylor & Francis Inc., 1900 Frost Road, Suite 101, Bristol, PA 19007

First published 1989

British Library Cataloguing in Publication Data

Learning to change: an LEA school-focused initiative.
  1. Great Britain. Schools. Curriculum. Development.
  Role of teachers
  I. Clough, Elizabeth II. Aspinwall, Kath III.
  Gibbs, Bob
  375'.00941

  ISBN 1-85000-630-X
  ISBN 1-85000-631-8 pbk

Library of Congress Cataloging in Publication Data

Learning to change : an LEA school-focused initiative / edited by
  Elizabeth Clough, Kath Aspinwall, and Bob Gibbs.
      p. cm.
    ISBN 1-85000-630-X. — ISBN 1-85000-631-8 (pbk.)
    1. Curriculum planning—England. 2. Teacher participation in
  curriculum planning—England. 3. School improvement programs—
  England. I. Clough, Elizabeth Engel. II. Aspinwall, Kath.
  III. Gibbs, Bob.
  LB1564.G7L43   1989
  375'.001'0942—dc20   89-36055
                                                            CIP

Jacket design by Annabel Jelley

Typeset in 11/13 Bembo
by Mathematical Composition Setters Ltd, Salisbury.

Printed in Great Britain by Taylor & Francis (Printers) Ltd., Basingstoke.

Contents

Contents

Preface

The relationship between LEAs and schools will be changed radically as the effects of the Education Reform Act begin to work through. The shift of power away from LEAs raises basic questions of their identity, role, even survival. This is the current context; it is not the context within which the Sheffield Curriculum Initiative (SCI) was launched in December, 1985. The then new Chief Education Officer, Bill Walton, proposed an authority-wide programme for the radical reform of the secondary curriculum in a letter to headteachers (see below). This letter clearly signalled that the motivation was concern for the quality of children's learning experiences in school and that any 'solutions', to be at all effective, must be conceived, developed and evaluated by teachers. For this to happen teachers would need time and support, a lot of both. The LEA decided to use most of its INSET monies to support teacher secondments, thus creating time for teachers to work on the reform collectively as well as individually. The powerful effect of the coming together of large numbers of teachers from both primary and secondary sectors (around 400 year-long secondments over three years) to work on curricular reform in Sheffield is difficult to convey. The overall purpose was LEA-wide, but individual schools set their own particular priorities for reform. These school-focused priorities, re-presented as school commissions (statements about areas for investigation and action), became the basis for the work of seconded teachers. Those out of school, primary teachers working as individuals and secondary teachers working in school teams (there were five teachers from each secondary school in the first year and two in subsequent years) needed to keep in touch with their colleagues in school. The dangers of dislocation, of ideas developed by teacher 'experts' outside school never reaching the parts that matter to bring about meaningful change in school, are well documented. A non-traditional secondment pattern was proposed to address this. Secondees spend approximately half of each week in school, not on timetable, but working with colleagues and students on commission development. The other half is spent on a

vii

planned in-service programme which both supports and extends teachers' understandings of the complexities of their commissions.

The various projects which go to make up SCI are not free-floating, independent ventures but are connected by common motivation and purpose made explicit in a set of principles which are outlined in Chapter 2. The chief components of SCI are the School-Focused Development Programme (SFD), the Curriculum and Assessment Resource (CAR) and the Management Support Team (MST). Although staff are attached to one of these projects they also work on others from time to time, so there is some interchange of staffing and exchange of ideas.

The school-focused secondment programme (SFS) (from its second year called SFD) constitutes the largest of the projects under SCI. Over a three year period each Sheffield secondary school has had nine full years' teacher secondments and fifty-three primary schools have each seconded one teacher to the programme. During the first year teachers were seconded in equal numbers to the LEA's two partnership institutions, Sheffield City Polytechnic and the University of Sheffield. They included teachers from the TVEI pilot institutions and from the four schools funded by the Lower Attaining Pupils Programme (LAPP), in Sheffield called the Curriculum Development Initiative (CDI). The CDI project adopted a different secondment pattern : teachers were seconded for one term each year over a three year period. After the first year a central LEA/University/Polytechnic team, comprising ten tutors (three of them part-time), was established to support secondees and to take responsibility for planning the programme. The CDI project remained separate from the SFD programme (though the principles on which it operates are very similar) and these teachers are supported by a small team of University and LEA advisory staff. During the first year of the programmes all teachers were enrolled on diploma courses at either the University or the Polytechnic. In subsequent years, when funding was no longer tied to registration on advanced programmes of study, this became an optional feature of secondment. Over the three years, then, substantial numbers of teachers have made use of their school-based work towards diploma and masters' awards.

The Curriculum and Assessment Resource (CAR) and the Management Support Team (MST), which were set up after the school-focused programme was established, met emerging authority-wide needs. Nine teachers were seconded to CAR in September 1987 with the task of developing a coherent LEA policy to implement the DES policy on recording achievement. A second group of seconded teachers within

CAR has been working on modular developments in the areas of technology, mathematics, humanities and creative arts. These tasks needed to be tackled at authority rather than school level. During the first year of SFS, evidence from the evaluation pointed to the need to provide effective support and development for headteachers and other senior staff in response to the school-focused programme. The MST was set up in January 1988 to respond to this need in the authority. More detail on the background and emerging practice within these two projects is given in Chapters 1 and 3 of this volume.

The structure of SCI is complex enough but still other educational interventions and initiatives have impinged on its evolution. It is not possible to mention them all but two new organizational features of the education service in Sheffield are particularly relevant.

In 1989 the LEA embarked on a major consultation with schools and colleges about its own organization and support structures – the outcome of this is not yet clear. However, for the last two years post-primary institutions, including special, have been arranged into eight geographical clusters, each acting as a forum for LEA/school debate on curricular and other issues. These clusters predated Sheffield's bid for TVEI-Extension monies (the authority enters TVEI-E in September 1989) but subsequently met the Training Agency's requirement for schools to work in consortia. Involvement in a wide range of activities, from INSET planning to pilot schemes for local financial management, is now organized on a cluster basis. Support for schools from SCI, either through SFD and CAR team members or through teacher secondments, is becoming more and more cluster based. Increasingly, primary INSET, including that associated with the National Curriculum and testing and other aspects of ERA, is being organized on a pyramid/cluster basis with the intention of improving links between the different stages of education.

In September 1988 eight new tertiary colleges opened in the city and three-quarters of secondary schools lost their sixth forms. Sheffield's proposal had been for a comprehensive post-16 provision but Keith Joseph, the then Secretary of State, intervened and eight schools in the south-west of the city were excluded from reorganization. The newly constituted tertiary colleges are not part of the secondment programme but, through clusters and in other ways, SCI engages with them.

Other initiatives, whilst not centrally within SCI, are linked to it and have been influenced by a similar philosophy. One such is the Sheffield Education Business Partnership (SEBP), formally established in January 1988 with a contract signed between the education service and the employer community in Sheffield, which sought to achieve 'better mutual understanding, support and co-operation'. Since then a small central team has been set up composed of individuals from business and education, and the partnership has supported a wide range of activities including school-focused and city-wide conferences and proposals for integrating work-related experience into the curriculum in a more systematic way across the city. The SEBP has acted as a focus for completion of a COMPACT feasibility study covering a wide range of community groups and this has led to the successful submission of a COMPACT proposal for all secondary schools. It is obvious that the work of the SEBP has links with the work carried out by CAR on the development of a Sheffield Record of Achievement and with school-focused developments around education/business co-operation.

In October 1986, a seconded teacher predicted that: 'The size and focus of the Initiative should mean that nothing is untouched and that no school is untouched. It will have a radical effect.' The evidence within this book suggests that this prophecy was not inaccurate. Schools have found that it is not possible to make changes in particular areas, for example in developing a Record of Achievement and Experience, without all kinds of accompanying changes in teaching style, student/teacher relationships, group arrangements and timetable patterns. The LEA has not been able to promote change in schools by becoming committed to a new relationship with schools without itself having to come to terms with change. The LEA is beginning to rethink its own behaviours and structures; it can only ask of schools what it is prepared to do for itself. The Education Reform Act of 1988 is of course giving further urgent impetus to the need for the various parts of the education service to examine their purposes and the nature of the relationships between them.

SCI is an evolving organism. The extensive evaluation activity around SCI (with a full-time evaluator and additional evaluation of the externally funded projects TVEI and CDI) has been designed principally to inform the learning which had to go on at so many levels if the project was to grow and flourish. Evaluation has been a properly integral part of the development of the initiative and its effects have been felt not only at LEA level but within schools and classrooms as teachers have taken on the task of evaluation as an essential part of school based developments. We decided not to commission a chapter on evaluation *per se* in this volume since this could give a distorted impression of the role evaluation has played within SCI. However, we are aware that some readers may be interested in generalized evaluation findings and a note on these is included as an endpiece to this volume.

In attempting to write about what has happened we have been conscious of the tension between the desire to record and explain the development of an interesting, possibly unique, project and the realization that we may find ourselves, as Stenhouse has it, 'placing firm boundaries on a continuous phenomena'. The writing of this book has therefore in itself been part of the process of developing our understanding of the complexity of what is taking place. In the pages that follow theory and practice are intermingled, some of the failures and limitations are expressed as well as much excitement and joy. We acknowledge that it is difficult to delineate SCI from some earlier influences and developments in Sheffield's educational history. However, the single most distinctive feature of SCI is the act of faith it places in teachers, a disposition not much in vogue in the 1980s but one which we believe has been more than justified by the developments over the last three years.

Elizabeth Clough, Kath Aspinwall, Bob Gibbs
Sheffield, May 1989

Acknowledgments

We are grateful to Jon Nixon of the University of Sheffield for his help and advice at the planning stage and to Bill Fisher of Barnsley LEA for commenting on an earlier draft of this volume.

CITY OF SHEFFIELD
EDUCATION DEPARTMENT
PO BOX 67
LEOPOLD STREET
SHEFFIELD
S1 1RJ

December 1985

Dear Colleague

THE FUTURE OF SHEFFIELD'S SECONDARY SCHOOLS

Within the prevailing model of comprehensive education Sheffield's secondary schools will bear comparison with any in the country. Examination results, pupil behaviour, atmosphere; they all indicate that our comprehensive schools have developed into caring well-managed and successful places of learning. And yet, there is increasing evidence that the time is right for a radical re-appraisal of the educational diet being offered in our schools.

The reorganization of secondary education on the basis of comprehensive schools was proposed in order to achieve the equality of educational opportunity which the previous system of organisation failed to achieve. There had been a disproportionate concentration of resources in the grammar schools and a relative lack of resources in the secondary modern schools: equality of access to resources and facilities was seen as fundamental to the notion of equality of opportunity.

There can be little doubt that the facilities and resources available in comprehensive schools are significantly better than those which were available in many run down inner-city secondary modern schools. And, of course, many more children are taking advantage of the access that they now have to those facilities and resources.

The implicit task which society set for the comprehensive school was to open up access to the grammar school curriculum to all our children. The main teaching task of the school thus remained pretty uncontroversial. Most comprehensive schools, like their grammar school predecessors, have concentrated on teaching traditional school subjects to examination level to as many of their pupils as possible. The vast majority of children still follow the single period – single subject –

single teacher organisation which was a characteristic of the grammar school. What schools are trying to teach is still based on assumptions of the academic curriculum of the traditional grammar school. (Such an implicit philosophy of education remains clearly divisive.)

There have, of course, been attempts to broaden and restructure the curriculum in our schools. Schools have developed programmes such as social and personal education, recreational activities and outdoor pursuits. These, however, have always been 'added on' extras. They rarely receive any form of accreditation in a system still dominated by public examinations. These developments are little more than attempts to enliven the curriculum by tinkering about at the margins; they rarely establish themselves with any credibility therefore in the education of our pupils.

It is becoming increasingly evident that not only *what* is taught, but *the way* in which it is taught needs radically re-thinking. School life is still too much about classrooms with one teacher trying to inform twenty-five pupils about an academic subject. Pupils still spend too much time sitting at their desks (supposedly) listening, reading and writing. One can easily understand why when this style of teaching, along with the curriculum and timetable, was inherited from the grammar school.

For the first time in generations the time is right for a radical change in what is offered to children. There is a growing realisation, both inside and outside education, that the curriculum and teaching styles of comprehensive schools no longer serve the needs of pupils. Certain aspects of the attitudes of the pupils reinforces such a view: absenteeism among pupils with little chance of examination success is high (particularly in later years), many pupils see no point in pursuing academic subjects in which they have no real chance of examination success, but most tellingly 65 per cent of pupils leave full time education as soon as the law allows.

What then should comprehensive education mean to Sheffield's children and their parents? It seems both uncontroversial and undeniable that our children are entitled to an education system which is interesting, significant and in touch with a wider reality on a day-to-day basis, as well as preparing them for adult life. A curriculum which directly seeks to meet the needs of the young adult in the late twentieth century must explicitly attempt to develop skills, competences and understanding. Such objectives can no longer remain assumed incidental corollaries of the process of knowledge transmission.

Curriculum domains (traditionally school subjects) need to be seen as mere structural devices in the furtherance of intelligence, capability, competence and humanity. They are not ends in themselves.

For schooling to become more enjoyable, it must become a more active, experiential and social process. More time must be spent in collaborative learning with pupils negotiating their own learning experiences. For schooling to become more significant, curriculum domains need to be interrelated in order that issues of current concern can be tackled. These issues of concern, e.g. economic awareness, information technology and personal development, must have a central expression in the curriculum. For the experience of children to be radically transformed, and be seen (by both pupil and teacher) to have been radically transformed, the assessment and monitoring of that experience can no longer be subcontracted to an examination system immersed in the 'cult of the fact'. Collaborative and experiential learning, economic awareness and an appreciation of information technology cannot be monitored by end-of-course written examinations. Records of Achievement and personal profiles provide a far more relevant portrayal of pupil experience.

The changes in the curriculum, the teaching style and the process of assessment that are necessary to transform the school experience of our children are so profound that they are too complex to be tackled within the traditional one or two year course with examinations at the end. It is the Authority's view that it is only by the modularisation of courses, together with their unit accreditation, that the revitalisation of the secondary curriculum becomes a manageable process.

Even so, no school can reasonably be expected to attempt in isolation the radical changes which are necessary.

Traditionally schools have (implicitly) been staffed and resourced on the assumption of 'no change' and the management role of the local authority has been predicated upon a low priority for innovation together with the effective maintenance of the status quo. This Authority is committed to a new relationship with schools and to major co-operative initiatives that will enable schools and teachers to make the radical changes necessary in adopting a modular curriculum.

A modular curriculum is incompatible with end-of-course GCSE examinations. However, separate Records of Achievement, unit accreditation of courses with schools becoming centres of accreditation for modular non-GCSE courses is manifestly divisive: more divisive, in fact, than any previous system. The Authority is in the process of negotiating with the Northern Examination Association a pilot integrated system of accreditation in which modular GCSE courses can be incorporated into Records of Achievement. This will facilitate the development of a modular curriculum with associated Records of Achievement for all pupils.

The Authority is, from this year, in receipt of additional resources from central government funding, i.e. TVEI, TRIST and LAPPS, which are being used to enhance and facilitate curriculum development initiatives which incorporate modularisation and accreditation.

By a major increase in the secondment programme the developments initiated above will be broadened to all curriculum domains and to schools across the Authority. The Authority is currently developing the joint concepts of a COMMISSIONING AGENT (operationally defined as the Advisory Service) and COMMISSIONED SECONDMENTS. By this process up to five teachers from each school will be specifically commissioned in a co-ordinated programme to develop, under tutorial support from either the University or the Polytechnic, the elements of the modular curriculum which will radically enhance the experience of our children.

Secondees will not be expected to work in isolation. They will, on the contrary, be expected to relate to each other on two levels. Firstly, all secondees from a given school will be commissioned by the Authority and will operate as a team with the brief to deliver a major joint contribution back to their school. Secondly, secondees from different (or maybe the same) school working in similar curriculum domains or on similar thru-curricular themes will be co-ordinated by the adviser responsible for that domain or theme. The products of their secondments will be fed into the Authority's Item Bank to be established for that purpose.

In order to facilitate the effective development of the secondment programme, some curriculum development teams (both domain related and theme related) must be brought into existence early next term and co-ordinated by the Advisory Service. Their function will be to begin the process of conceptualising the implications of, and establishing the parameters for, the commissioned secondment programme starting in September 1986.

The issues which must be faced by teachers are daunting in both their size and their complexity. Their resolution is dependent upon an unparalleled degree of openness and co-operation between schools, the Authority and the local institutions of higher education. Teachers will need the support, interest and involvement of the Authority if they are to have any hope of success in their endeavours to redefine the process of schooling.

Your sincerely,

W. S. Walton
Chief Education Officer

Introduction

The contributions to the first part of this book outline the context, principles and something of the practice of the Sheffield Curriculum Initiative. In Chapter 1 Roy Hedge and Bill Walton set the scene with a discussion of how the various components of the initiative came into being and of the beliefs and concerns, educational and political, which motivated it. The chapter signals an interesting tension between the initiation and conceptualization of innovation from 'the top' and the practice of devolvement of both the responsibility and the power to teachers to bring about change in schools.

In Chapter 2 the principles which underpin the Initiative are spelled out; they apply to all projects within SCI though most examples are taken from the school-focused in-service programmes. Thus, particular conceptions of learning and equal opportunities are outlined as key principles of SCI. In addition, curriculum development is understood as inseparable from the human relationships which bring it about. This leads to an interpretation of INSET which seeks to forge and exploit the complex connections between curriculum development, staff development and the development of the school as an organization. Curricula are reviewed and changed not in isolation but in context. There is no suggestion that the ideas about learning, equal opportunities or INSET, which underpin SCI, were recently invented in Sheffield; rather that in combination, and through making them explicit, a distinctive framework of values has emerged.

In Chapter 3 three separate accounts offer glimpses of how the vision and the principles have guided practice. Douglas Finlayson's piece gives a flavour of the work of the Management Support Team; Jeanie Hedge and Colin Martin offer a cameo from the work of the Curriculum and Assessment Resource; Daryl Agnew and Carole Goodwin describe part of the SFD out of school programme. All the authors in this chapter have chosen to exemplify the enormous variety of work within SCI by focusing on processes and ways of working rather than on structures and organizational parameters.

In Part Two further examples of the practical effects of the Initiative follow and insight is offered into the thinking and working of three of the groups of people centrally involved in the carrying out of the SCI developments. In Chapter 4 Ian Anniss and Bob Gibbs reflect on the principles, highlight guidelines and define the role of the school tutor in the SFD tutorial team. They unravel and illuminate the many different aspects of their work, outlining the complexities, explaining what they do and how, and why they do it in this way. In conclusion they consider the implications for all those who are, or wish to be, involved in supporting school focused development.

In Chapter 5 two of the SFD secondees recount their personal experience of their year's secondment. They describe the carrying out of their school commissions, how they related to their colleagues, their sense of professional and personal development and the way their work is continuing on their return to full-time teaching. At the beginning and end of the chapter these two individual accounts are set into the context of the wider evaluation of the work of secondees which has been carried out by the LEA SCI evaluator.

Chapter 6 offers the combined perspectives of four secondary and one primary headteacher representing the different elements of SCI. For heads, the SCI initiative is but one part of a plethora of sometimes confusing or even contradictory developments, some of which are being nationally imposed. The tensions they feel themselves to be facing are reflected in the chapter, which makes it clear that developments can have both intended and unintended consequences. Heads feel responsible for maintaining a balance whilst at the same time wishing to devolve at least some of their power within their schools. The chapter ends with the heads looking forward to building a new relationship with the LEA and the community in the new context created by the ERA.

The third part of this volume draws upon challenging contributions from three outside perspectives: the view from Europe, from higher education and from other LEAs. The authors' reflections and commentaries upon the Sheffield Curriculum Initiative raise important implications and fundamental issues for the wider educational community as it engages in the process of change and development.

The author of Chapter 7 is Fritz Bohnsack, Professor of Education at the University of Essen, who has been engaged in research on school-focused developments in the United Kingdom and West

Germany. As part of that research he has spent a substantial proportion of the last year closely attached to SCI, in particular the SFD programme. This chapter takes an interesting and thought provoking view of SCI addressing the central issues of education for democracy and global responsibility, the concept of 'good' schools and effective in-service support for teachers and schools. It brings a fresh dimension to the problems and challenges facing education in Western Europe now and in the future.

In Chapter 8, Peter Clough of the University of Sheffield writes from the advantageous position of having a knowledge and understanding of SCI. The changes in INSET resourcing have radically altered the relationship between higher education, schools and LEAs. In a refreshing and stimulating way, the chapter uncovers and explores the nature and magnitude of these changes by addressing issues around the areas of learning, assessment, knowledge, power and equality of opportunity. In a critically reflective way, this chapter highlights some of the opportunities, demands and tensions placed upon higher education and the implications for the wider educational community.

Tim Brighouse brings a particularly useful perspective on SCI in Chapter 9. His background and reputation eminently qualify him to focus on issues which LEAs will have to respond to as change and reform demanded by the Education Reform Act gathers pace and momentum. The emphasis and understanding placed on qualities of leadership, shared vision, opportunism and developing a strategy for change, bring sharply into focus crucial areas of concern that LEAs have little choice but to address. The chapter offers an analysis of educational change over recent years against the backcloth of social, economic and political realities. The conclusions give important insights and a potential sense of direction as education moves into the post-ERA world.

Part One
Starting Points

1
The Vision and the Context

Roy Hedge and Bill Walton

The Sheffield Curriculum Initiative represents the efforts of one LEA to make collective sense of the paradoxical and turbulent world of schooling. In a decade in which radical right and left alike have subjected venerated institutions and axioms to extravagant critique, education has sometimes seemed in danger of losing its way entirely. The purposes, methods, governance and finance of schools are themselves matters of deep controversy, inextricably linked with political struggles. Acute and often painful social and economic change has transformed the climate within which schools operate in a city like Sheffield. Power over crucial aspects of the system is shifting. The clients of the system, pupils, parents, employers and the community at large are themselves changing and being changed by their aspirations of and participation in education as well as by the wider cultural turmoil of the times in which we live.

Secondary schools and teachers have had a rough ride in recent years. Jim Callaghan's 'Great Debate' was widely understood within schools as a condemnation of current practice in the late 1970s. The 1980s have been fertile in swingeing criticism of what schools do. Early in the decade, industry and the MSC were to the fore in demands for a more vocationally orientated curriculum and as part of the argument schools were blamed for Britain's poor economic performance. It is interesting to note the absence of congratulation now that this performance is deemed to be transformed. At the same time, it was argued by the right that basic standards in the three R's were declining under the weight of time given to new, trendy social education. Meanwhile, from other quarters came demands that schools should cure newly diagnosed social ills through political education, social education, health education, moral education, environmental education, peace education etc.

The most recent reaction to this confusion, at least as represented by the actions of the present government through the introduction of GCSE and subsequently the National Curriculum, has been to try to cut through the debate by a determined movement to re-establish the primacy of traditional school subjects and reduce the ways of examining them by the abolition of CSE and the virtual elimination of Mode 3. All of this, remember, was taking place against a background of fierce strife within the profession over teachers' pay and conditions of service, culminating in an imposed contract, specified hours and loss of teachers' national negotiating rights. These difficult years coincided with a disastrous fall in pupil numbers (a very high 38 per cent in Sheffield) because of the collapse in the birth rate, with the inevitable and painful consequence of redeployment of staff and falling school incomes. Teachers felt blamed and undervalued. It was against this background of change and the need for a response from the LEA that SCI was born.

Sheffield is not the place it was, though we make the statement as one of fact and not of nostalgic yearning for a mythical unproblematical past. About two-thirds of Sheffield's pupils were still leaving full-time education as soon as the law allowed, some informally even before that. The collapse of the steel industry in the early 1980s left us with a situation where only 10 per cent of 16-year old school leavers went to jobs. The effect on pupil morale and motivation seemed potentially disastrous. It seemed that the problems of secondary schools in particular would demand urgent support for teachers and their efforts, if the quality of educational provision were to be maintained or enhanced.

It is hardly surprising that the dearth of job opportunities should have been accompanied by a perceived fall-off in pupil motivation, particularly in the crucial last two years of compulsory schooling. This was widely reported by teachers. The steady improvement in examination results across the city was halted. It is true, of course, that accounts of pupil resistance to learning are as old as organized teaching, but teachers, LEA officers and advisers all felt that a qualitative change was under way. Vandalism and open hostility from pupils were increasing. Indifference to the value of school work seemed to many experienced teachers to be on the increase across a broad spectrum of pupils as the social rewards for all but the highest academic achievements became devalued at 16-plus.

Not all of the underachievement of secondary pupils can be blamed on economic set-backs in the life of the city or on the particular traumas facing education. Wider changes in society have made traditional teaching less possible. The values espoused by young people (and often their parents too) have shifted considerably over the last generation, with support for the values of authority, obedience and acceptance weakened. Pupils experience relative autonomy outside school much earlier than did their parents' generation. A major feature of youth culture is the pressure towards instant gratification. 'Boring' is the ultimate negative. Slick instant entertainment from computers and television make lessons at school seem pale and thin by comparison. These changes in pupils' worlds and minds must mean that schools have to adapt to a new reality if they are to maintain their impact as key learning institutions. For too many pupils the learning available in the secondary school has come to seem imposed, arcane and detached from a wider social reality. Where merely average examination results are not a marketable commodity there must be a powerful premium on the intrinsic interest or worth of what schools offer.

The curriculum offerings of our schools, however well-intentioned and caringly constructed, do not seem to grip the attention and fire the excitement of ordinary youngsters. It is much easier to criticize the standard curriculum for its failure to motivate pupils than to specify an uncontroversially successful alternative. Nevertheless, some directions do seem to be clear. Particularly striking is the way in which the value of learning has come to be perceived and explained in the schooling industry. Learning and the achievement of 'results' seem to have become inextricably confused. Education has been reduced largely to the accumulation of knowledge and technique in pursuit of examination goals and principally justified instrumentally – in terms of access to better jobs and social success. 16-plus examination results are a key social placement mechanism. Is it any surprise that when better than average success in these examinations does not lead to social success in the current economic situation, then the enterprise seems hollow to the participants? In our anxiety to sell the value of the examined results of successful school experience to our pupils, we have lost sight of the power of personal learning. In so doing we have encouraged pupils to see learning merely as a way of getting results, preferably by the least effort. This is a far cry from attempting the induction of our pupils into the idea of learning's intrinsic excitement and value, as part of the business of coming to an understanding of themselves and their world.

In spite of the curriculum projects of the 60s and 70s and an obvious loosening of the social order in many schools through the widespread abolition of school uniforms and corporal punishment, what schools offer is still recognizably the same as a generation earlier.

The timetable is still constructed with the same building blocks of traditional school subjects as it was in the grammar schools of the 1950s. The demands of recent years have produced marginal changes, such as the time given to careers and social education and some experimentation in classroom style with the introduction of more individual and group work. There is more talk and a little less chalk but the classroom and its rituals would still be readily recognized by the parents of today's pupils. In practice, the historic mission of the comprehensive school has been the attempt to make the grammar school curriculum accessible to all.

Against this background, one of the key directions informing SCI has come to be the drive to render experience of school more attractive to ordinary pupils. Where extrinsic motivation is threatened an extra premium has to be put on the perceived intrinsic interest and value of the curriculum for pupils. If pupils find school boring and if the instrumental rewards for overcoming the boredom, except for the gifted few, are more hoped for than real, then we must work harder than before to make that which schools offer more attractive and motivating. Even if it were not the case that the end rewards of moderate success at school are in temporary local decline, we should still be committed as an education service to the value of learning for its own sake and be seeking every possible opportunity to enhance pupils' lives and futures through their accumulation of knowledge, under-standing, sensitivity and competence. SCI is underpinned by the notion that the learner has to be personally engaged in learning, to see its importance and particular relevance to personal growth, if it is to be profoundly effective. This spirit of starting 'where the learner is at' and pursuing educational objectives through the medium of the learner's interests is central to the INSET programmes within SCI. It is no less of an important insight in terms of the common experience of pupils.

If intrinsic motivation is as crucial for successful learning as we suspect, then there are features of the usual school curriculum which must be deeply dysfunctional in terms of pupil access to the oppor-tunity to maximize what they get from school learning. Based as it is on school subjects derived from the ways in which the academic com-munity classifies and taxonomizes formal knowledge, the curriculum has become divorced from and dissonant with the out-of-school experience of all but a handful of pupils. Life is not divided into school subjects. In this sense we see the central thrust of the National Curriculum, with its setting of traditionally defined subjects in curriculum concrete as the hardcore subject matter of schools, as profoundly retrogressive. It leaves untouched, or makes even more difficult, the teacher's problem of seriously engaging young people in real learning. If we seek to make the access of pupils to learning easier, then we should be relaxing not tightening the rules of engagement which define the entry points to knowledge which pupils and teachers can use. The abolition of CSE, the tightening hold of centralizing agencies on the approval of qualifications and the grip of examination board bureaucracies on pupils' educational experience have made the teacher's task of engaging reluctant pupils all the more difficult. We would look in the future to radical schemes of curriculum reconstruction, moving away from tight subject-based definitions of what is educationally worthwhile knowledge towards modular structures with multiple entry points.

There is a further point to be made about the definition of school learning through traditional subjects in that it removes the setting of learning objectives from the learner in what is a profoundly alienating process. Pupils' experience of learning is that it is defined in its objectives, methods and outcomes by somebody else and has little to do with their own interests or indeed with themselves as people. The experience of school for the learner is too often rooted in powerlessness. To be powerless but accepting of the situation, as was the common fate of pupils a generation earlier, is one thing: to be powerless and resentful is another, and an unlikely context for successful learning. When this experience of schooling is set alongside young people's growing autonomy beyond school with less supervision, more freedom and control over their lives and a failing sense of trust in the adult world to provide a future of security, safety and optimism, then alienation from school learning starts to look like a rational reaction.

Curriculum and staff development did not suddenly begin in Sheffield with the unveiling of SCI. Many schools have used the provision of INSET resources through SFD to advance changes already devised before 1986. Concern to improve the quality of schooling was equally widespread. Nevertheless, our unease about the appropriateness of much secondary school provision led us to consider ways of making a major intervention in the system, to initiate a debate and to stimulate action to reassess and improve our provision. Later chapters outline much of what followed. It is always tempting to endow the past with more coherence than was the case and in so doing to pretend to an unrealistic wisdom and prescience. We were guided by a powerful unease about the structure and content of the secondary curriculum and doubts about the conventional social organization of schools. Further, we became committed to greater curriculum relevance and a recognition of more pupil autonomy in both the generation and assessment of learning goals. At the same time we came to see that although the problems facing primary schools seemed less urgent, they were no less important. There is often a significant gap between the celebratory rhetoric surrounding practice in primary education and the reality of actual schools. It seemed reasonable to begin a modest programme of working with a small number of primary schools alongside the major thrust in the secondary sector. We had no clear idea of the outcomes of reform but did have unconditional commitment to ways of working, by engaging schools and teachers and if possible the wider community in a partnership with the LEA to investigate then invigorate our provision.

The educational experiences of pupils are organized by teachers. Teachers, it is true, work within many constraints and, even before the advent of the National Curriculum, were not free to devise curriculum and teaching style unfettered. Certainly for most pupils beyond 14 years, syllabuses are defined by examination boards. Nevertheless, it remains the case that the day-to-day classroom business is teacher designed. It seems axiomatic then that the teacher must be the starting point for review and change. We determined to use the possibilities of in-service training to engage with teachers in a reappraisal of classroom practice. The School Focused Secondment programme was our first foray. Announced in December 1985, this gave each secondary school the opportunity to second five teachers for a year to research and implement a commission or series of commissions on behalf of their school. Our TVEI Pilot and LAPP projects came at about the same time and were similarly based on teacher secondment. Changes in funding opportunities have led to a reduction to two per school in subsequent years. Much of the fascinating detail of how this programme has developed in three years is outlined in later chapters. It is important from the outset to understand some of the principles which have informed the evolution of this programme.

We were initially awed by the magnitude and ambition of the task we were setting. There is an elephants' graveyard of grand curriculum developments of the 1960s and '70s. Both our own local experience of curriculum development projects and the published evidence suggested to us that the key to success again lay with teachers. The organization of pupils' learning is an intensely personal affair, resting for its quality substantially on the sensitivity, wit and knowledge of teachers. Teachers' commitment, nervous energy and determination have to be harnessed if change is to be successfully implemented. The principle of teacher ownership of change is crucial to SFD and wider SCI developments. If teachers do not feel the need to change, or see change as something imposed, then they will resist. Grand designs from outside experts offer teachers only the role of implementer. Often the teachers on the receiving end of well-meaning innovations have had no stake in the success of the planned change but have had the responsibility for achieving it. For teachers, as for pupils, we came back again to the conclusion that learning, especially that which produces changes in behaviour, must take the agenda of the learner as its starting point.

The SFD programmes have been designed to address the need for change by taking the agendas of schools and secondees as starting points. The commissions which secondees have sought to develop have been the media through which their learning has been facilitated. The concerns of schools and teachers have also been taken seriously in the work of CAR and the Management Support Team. Over three years, SCI has developed a radical and consistent in-service model; it depends crucially on the notion that learning which leads to actual change in schools and the enhancement of the lives of pupils will not take place unless teachers feel that their needs are being addressed and that they have substantial control over the direction of their learning. On the SFD programme particularly, where teachers are seconded for at least a term, and usually a year, recognition has been given to the need for personal growth, for reflective activity and the need for supportive learning groups. The kind of learning which changes classroom behaviour and challenges traditional relationships is necessarily personal as well as professional. It often depends on learning new things about oneself and on successfully reflecting on personal experience in new ways. The challenge presented within supportive groups, where that challenge is heard without threat and the role of the tutor is as critical friend rather than expert, have encouraged us to develop the programme increasingly along these lines. This style of work with teachers, depending on the role of skilled facilitation by SCI staff to establish a climate which supports high levels of participation and trust in working groups, has become a main feature of the work of SFD, CAR and the Management Support Team. Teachers have a wealth of experience of schools and pupils. In such working groups they can come to unlock that experience, reflect upon it and lay the foundations for changing their personal practice.

We should emphasize, though, that affording respect to the experience and expertise of teachers does not imply a wholly neutral, laissez-faire or anarchic stance. SCI does represent a sense of direction and a set of common values expressed through the processes employed by the component parts. It does not advocate or prescribe an obligatory course of action for schools, neither does it seek to impose a detailed blueprint for change. The consistency lies in the promotion of reflection on experience as a means of illuminating practice and formulating action. For SCI staff themselves the experience of the last three years has been one of important personal and professional learning, and responding to the LEA evaluations, they have adapted and refined the structures and processes of the INSET programmes.

During the first year of the school-focused programme it became apparent that our basic strategy of enabling schools to help themselves through teacher secondment would need further refinement. We were struck particularly by the way in which much attempted curricular reform foundered on the rocks of assessment processes. In the world before Standard Assessment Tasks (SATs), GCSE represented the system's basic pupil assessment mechanism. Our attempts as an LEA to pilot modular GCSE submissions through an examination board, pioneered by our TVEI Pilot and a technology project at CAR, had illustrated the difficulty and time-consuming frustrations of that process. In any case, the pronouncements of the DES and SEC and more recently SEAC are profoundly discouraging for those who see this as a route to curriculum reform. We determined to mount a major project to devise and implement a Record of Achievement and Experience for Sheffield pupils. In this we were encouraged by DES statements, as we have been by the reports of the Record of Achievement National Steering Committee and the Pilot Record of Achievement in Schools Evaluation team. (*Records of Achievement: A Statement of Policy*, DES and Welsh Office, 1984; *RANSC Interim Report*, 1987; *RANSC Final Report*, 1989; *Records of Achievement, Report of the National Evaluation of Pilot Schemes*, PRAISE, 1989.) In addition there was our own conviction that the valuing of pupil experience and the inclusion of the learner in goal setting could be best advanced through a system of recording achievement which went far beyond the externally-defined objectives model of public examinations. We envisaged a system which would be curriculum driven, pupil-centred rather than objectives led and which would seek to value and celebrate all of a pupil's experience, not just that recognized by examination boards. The widespread allegiance to such principles in secondary schools could go a long way towards transforming the relationships between teachers and pupils.

Clearly no school could create a Record of Achievement and Experience (RAE) for the whole city on its own. Equally clearly, for the LEA to devise a record and attempt to secure the enthusiastic participation of schools at a later stage would deny many of the principles outlined above. The Curriculum and Assessment Resource (CAR) came into being to facilitate the creation of a RAE and to pilot the production of a series of modular GCSE courses. The task of the teachers seconded to CAR's RAE panel was to work with schools in order to devise a RAE largely acceptable to teachers over a period of time. Some of CAR's work is detailed later (see Chapter 3) but its key characteristic is its way of working. There was no RAE blueprint to begin with, merely a set of principles. CAR began with a brief to conduct a campaign in schools to raise awareness of RAE issues and to facilitate the sharing of experience of practice. It later conducted two very extensive formal consultations and only produced recommendations after almost two years of work with schools and teachers, safe in the knowledge that wide understanding and enthusiasm for the outcomes already existed in schools in anticipation of the production of the actual document. Once again there was the attempt to prepare the climate for and to establish ownership of a projected innovation through grassroots participation within a sense of direction initiated by the LEA.

A lacuna in our thinking rapidly emerged in the first year of the programme. Seconding five teachers, even with the full involvement of the school in the identification of their curricular priorities, clearly placed some stress on the ability of the school as an organization to cope with the challenge. It seemed that we had created a responsibility to provide broader support for the system just as headteachers in particular were trying to deal with a whole barrage of problems, not least of which was teachers' industrial action. The further stress on schools caused by having five missionary advocates suddenly in their midst and the difficulties of managing the tensions caused by the quickening pace of change clearly pointed out for us what we dimly realised already: that our provision of support for headteachers was dismal. The work of the Management Support Team grew from this realization that not only was curriculum development unlikely in the absence of staff and personal development but that the support and development of the management of schools was equally vital. Again, some of the work of the MST is described below (see Chapter 3). It is important here to show how the MST fits in to the sense of direction which permeates SCI.

Management training for headteachers, no doubt stimulated by the advent of local management of schools, is much in vogue. Most of what seems to be available focuses on teaching headteachers new skills. Without denying that this may be necessary, our own efforts have concentrated on responding to what headteachers perceive as their own needs for support. With the invaluable help of a consultant, a group of seconded headteachers, supported by CAR and SFD staff, have begun to work with their colleagues in ways which closely mirror the style of other elements in SCI, concentrating on helping heads to reflect in honest and realistic ways on their experience and, with expert facilitation, to begin to derive support from sharing problems and dilemmas.

From the beginning we have attempted to manage the various parts of SCI in a way consistent with our style of working with teachers. LEA administration have many of the features of big bureaucracies. They are hierarchically organized, often with long chains of command. Innovations advocated from the top can meet with huge resistance from below as staff conceive of themselves as implementers of other people's goals rather than active and willing participants in change. Innovative practice is difficult to stimulate from below because of the vested interests of powerful groups within the organization in the maintenance of the status quo. There is plenty of politics. We wanted key SCI staff to enjoy considerable freedom to develop radical models of staff development to meet the new challenges we were throwing down. For two years now the CAR and SFD teams have operated in a context where status distinctions have been minimized despite differences in pay. Both of these teams comprise staff seconded from other posts and this has in some ways been a major difficulty in so far as it generates intense annual anxiety about their personal futures. Nevertheless, non-hierarchical and non-bureaucratic team work has become a major feature of the SCI landscape. The various ways of working with teachers have been generated within the teams through discussion and reflection. Jobs are shared and the excitement and involvement generated within these teams have been intense. There has been a conscious attempt to establish a climate of mutual support and non-threatening challenge within the teams. There have, of course, been disagreements and not all of these are always resolved. The general style of work has evolved on the basis of shared understanding of and allegiance to a constantly shifting consensus based on experience.

SCI was initiated in 1986, so predating the debate on the National Curriculum and the Education Reform Act of 1988. The principles and directions of SCI were set by our reaction to our own situation within the LEA. When the outlines of government thinking became clear it seemed that their sense of direction was fundamentally different from ours, particularly in the attempt to legislate change from the top. As more details become clear, however, it seems all the more important that we started when and where we did. Section 1 of the Education Reform Act states:

> The curriculum for a maintained school satisfies the require-ments of this section if it is a balanced and broadly based curriculum which –
>
> a) promotes the spiritual, moral, cultural, mental and physical development of pupils at the school and of society; and
>
> b) prepares such pupils for the opportunities, respon-sibilities and experiences of adult life. (ERA: Part 1, p 1.).

These principles also represent the aspirations of SCI. The task of schools and LEAs in implementing the National Curriculum remain unchanged, namely the provision for pupils of access to learning. It is difficult to see how teachers can make a full response to the high aspirations of Part 1 of the Act without a programme of support such as that represented by SCI. A smooth implementation of the Education Reform Act can only proceed where the culture of schools is already responsive to the idea of learning to change in order to offer pupils the highest quality provision.

SCI is the product of a very large number of Sheffield's teachers and LEA staff. The participation of Sheffield University and Sheffield City Polytechnic, especially in the early days, was important. It has evolved rapidly and become increasingly sophisticated in its appli-cations over a very short period of time. There is still a long way to go especially in terms of widening the educational partnership to include parents, business and the wider community in the educational debate. We believe, however, that a start has been made in the effort to encourage a new climate based on the values of a learning culture, in which realistic innovative response to the challenge of changing needs can be met without fear.

Roy Hedge and Bill Walton

References

DEPARTMENT OF EDUCATION AND SCIENCE (1984) *Records of Achievement: A Statement of Policy*, London, HMSO.
DEPARTMENT OF EDUCATION AND SCIENCE (1987) *Records of Achievement National Steering Committee: Interim Report*, London, HMSO.
DEPARTMENT OF EDUCATION AND SCIENCE (1989) *Records of Achievement National Steering Committee: Report*, London, HMSO.
DEPARTMENT OF EDUCATION AND SCIENCE (1989) *Records of Achievement, Report of the National Evaluation of Pilot Schemes*, London, HMSO.
DEPARTMENT OF EDUCATION AND SCIENCE (1989) *Education Reform Act, 1988*, London, HMSO.

2
Principles Guiding Change

Kath Aspinwall, Elizabeth Clough and Rosie Grant

This chapter describes three essential principles behind the work of the Sheffield Curriculum Initiative (SCI); subsequent chapters offer some insights into how these principles have been translated into the practical efforts of those trying to achieve change. We do not claim that these principles in themselves are unique to SCI but, in combination, they provide a distinctive framework which guides the great variety of activity taking place under the SCI umbrella. Firstly, there is a recognition that the programme for reform in schools must attend to the purposes and processes of learning in schools as well as to curricular content. In the past, many attempts at both curricular and assessment reform have proceeded without recourse to any detailed reflection on the nature of learning – this probably for the very understandable reason that such reflection raises questions which are both unfamiliar and difficult. The belief that better learning follows more or less automatically from the revision of curricular materials and adjustments to teaching methods implies acceptance of a transmission model of learning. The learning of both students and teachers is thus, at least by implication, considered to be both predictable and unproblematic. Much curriculum development of the 1960s and 70s appears to have been based on this assumption. In this chapter we elaborate an alternative model of learning on which work under SCI is based and indicate ways in which questions of students' and teachers' learning have been explicitly addressed.

A second key principle is that of equality of opportunity; this has been identified as a unifying construct for work under SCI. The interpretation is a broad one and includes not only race and gender, but class and disability in various forms. Support for change in schools under SCI addresses questions of equality of opportunity in a number of ways: through the content and processes of the in-service provision as well as through issues of curricular access and teaching and learning approaches in schools. The argument for the permeation of equal opportunities work within the initiative is elaborated later in this chapter. It is a bold approach, rarely attempted within such a large initiative.

The ways in which all those who work in a school relate to one another within the organization profoundly affect the school's capacity for change. The third principle is that only an integrated model of in-service recognizes the fundamental point that curricular change in schools is achieved only when proper attention is given to the development of staff understanding of the change and the organizational context in which that occurs. Some previous INSET has focused on one of these aspects of development to the exclusion, or partial exclusion, of the rest. For example, some initiatives have been curriculum-led and relied on the dissemination of materials produced by groups of teacher 'experts'. Other forms of INSET have focused exclusively on the personal and professional development of individual teachers; many LEA short courses, diploma and masters' programmes at universities and polytechnics and management training courses would fit into this category. Frequently, such in-service investment has been seen as the starting point for wider institutional change, but in practice this 'spill over' into the life of the school has failed to materialize. In-service work under SCI encourages classroom teachers, as well as headteachers, to consider the organizational context and to challenge approaches to the management of change as an integral part of their work.

Teachers and Students as Learners

From the outset of SCI there was a recognition that solutions to problems of curriculum and assessment were conditional upon exploration of an understanding of the nature of learning. Thus, the CEO'S letter (Walton, 1985) proposed that, alongside a re-examination of content, Sheffield schools needed to ask more fundamental questions about why and how that content was taught and learnt.

During the 1980s some important curricular initiatives, such as TVEI, have highlighted the centrality of learning processes in curricular reform (see Clough, Clough and Nixon, 1989). The reasons for this shift of emphasis is a matter for speculation – they are no doubt many and various. Evidence of 'non-learning', that is of a large gap between a teacher's intentions and learners' understandings, is detectable from a number of different sources, for example from observational work in classrooms (Armstrong, 1980; Rowland, 1984), from national monitoring programmes (Assessment of Performance Unit reports), from studies of children's conceptions (Driver, 1983; Hughes, 1986) and from evaluations of curriculum development projects (Nuffield Science etc.). But a further crucial strand of influence seems to have been at work in shifting the curricular focus in the learner's direction. The burgeoning of 'vocationally relevant' courses in post-16 training and in programmes of study for 14-16 year olds (e.g., TVEI, BTEC, SCIP, YTS, CPVE etc.), have been accompanied by a much sharper focus on student learning and its assessment. In these courses there is a requirement for precision in observation and recording of learning outcomes, personal and social as well as practical and cognitive. The imperative for such precision about what a student has learnt is in marked contrast to the traditional external examination system which offers a single norm-related grading of performance. Some commentators (e.g., Hargreaves, 1986; Stronach, 1988; Brown and Ashton, 1987) have suggested that this new style of assessment could well be motivated by an intention to use education as an instrument of social determination and control, rather than by purely pedagogic concerns.

In this account, we want simply to record that a shift towards 'student-centred learning' appears to have permeated important parts of the system and to have reached the consciousness of many teachers. However, many of the materials which have been produced to support teachers in their endeavours to move towards a more student-centred approach offer strategies and practical 'how-to-do-it' advice without any deeper exploration of underpinning values and learning theories (Easen, 1985; Hunt and Hitchin, 1985). We believe that a strategic approach is likely to produce real classroom change only if it is accompanied by some re-thinking on the part of teachers about what it means to learn.

Later in this section, we will indicate ways in which challenges to the traditional transmission model of learning have been incorporated into activities with teachers and students under SCI. This theme will be further exemplified in Chapter 3.

As a preliminary, we see the need to set out the assumptions about learning which SCI tutors and trainers subscribe to – not a straightforward task, given that we come from a variety of backgrounds, each with its own tradition and influences. However, we recognize that we have drawn on ideas from cognitive and social psychology (the theories of Piaget, 1973; Kelly, 1955; Ausubel, 1978 and Donaldson, 1978, for example), on the writings of those with a declared humanistic, even therapeutic interest (e.g. Maslow, 1968; Rogers, 1969) and on the work of those who have applied these ideas quite explicitly to a pedagogic context (Freire, 1972; Bruner, 1966; Driver, 1983; Ferguson, 1982, etc.). Below we outline a view of learning which differs from a passive transmission model in a number of crucial and interrelated respects.

(1) An Active Construction of Meaning

Learning (of both students and teachers) is an active process of construction of meaning – both the locus of control and the responsibility for evaluation of the usefulness and relevance of learning lies with the individual learner. This tenet carries implications for the power relationship between student and teacher and for the management of learning opportunities in and out of the classroom.

(2) Interaction with Prior Experience

Learning is interactional and can occur only as the learner makes sense of particular experiences in particular contexts. This 'making sense' involves connecting with an individual's prior knowledge and experience. Thus, new learning has to relate to, and ultimately 'fit with', what individuals already understand. The notion of interaction does not carry any prescriptions about teaching and learning strategies since such interaction may be observably 'active', or it may be less observable such as listening or reading.

(3) The Context of Learning

Consideration of the context of learning – the characteristics of the learning environment – must take account, not only of the presentation of curricular materials and the management of groups of learners, but of the feelings and emotions of the participants towards both the learning task and themselves. For learners to believe in and be changed by what they learn, as distinct from being able to reproduce the ideas, the 'affective' component of learning must be recognized, valued and utilized throughout the learning process. Broadening the notion of 'context' in this way extends the legitimate forum for learning beyond the classroom, to the whole school and the surrounding community.

(4) Learning Involves Change

Learning is always provisional in the sense that most of what is 'learned' is subject to occasional if not frequent revision in the light of changing circumstances. Change in understanding may involve a basic restructuring of ideas or, alternatively, an extension of the learner's existing ideas. In either case, there is the clear implication that we need to create non-threatening settings which encourage learners to experiment and to be creative and intuitive, as well as to be reflective and self-critical.

The model of learning sketched briefly above is demonstrated in various aspects of the development work under SCI – in the way in which seconded headteachers have worked with colleagues within the Management Support Team (MST), the central focus on learning within the development of a Sheffield Record of Achievement and Experience by the Curriculum and Assessment Resource (CAR), the planned experiences of seconded teachers within the School-Focused Development (SFD) programme and the incorporation of these ideas into curriculum development work in schools. A specific example from work within SFD is sketched below.

Four days of the twelve-day SFD induction programme at the beginning of the year are devoted to an exploration of the nature of learning. A student tracking exercise makes the focal point for this work; successive cohorts of secondees have reported this to be one of the most influential experiences of the year. Teachers first spend some time reflecting on their own significant learning experiences and sharing the details, the conditions and the feelings which surrounded these. Some commonalities emerge and many teachers are surprised to discover that good learning experiences were frequently unplanned and unanticipated, that emotions and feelings were very important in determining learning outcomes, indeed that boundaries between personal and professional learning are often far from sharp. For the tracking exercise teachers work in a school other than their own, sometimes secondary teachers exchange with primary teachers. They spend a whole day with a student, with the aim of experiencing a day's schooling from the student's perspective. The focus is on learning, not on teaching. Teacher and student discuss the events of the day when school finishes and this is audio recorded. Armed with field notes and tapes the secondees then try to make sense of their data and share their thoughts and feelings about what they have learnt with other secondees and with tutors. In the final one-day seminar, secondees are guided in systematic and critical exploration of the experience towards addressing the question 'What have I learned about learning?' This has generated many hundreds of verbal and written observations from the testimony of some 160 teachers over a two-year period. These amount to a view of learning which bears great similarity to the model outlined above. We have arranged some typical points from teachers into four groupings which match and support the four points above.

(1) An Active Construction of Meaning

— learning is process, not product
— learning is controlled by students
— learning does not follow automatically from good teaching
— learning is difficult to recognize and assess
— teacher expectations are different from student outcomes

(2) Interaction with Prior Experience

— learning involves relating present to previous experience
— tasks must be meaningful to individuals
— learning depends on learners' interests and energies
— learning involves challenge, individually defined
— teaching must start where the student is at

(3) The Context of Learning

— 'good' learning contexts are not easily definable
— the classroom climate, its atmosphere, is so important
— good relationships are vital for learning
— group dynamics affect learning
— learning is influenced by the physical environment

(4) Learning Involves Change

— learning is not an 'all or nothing' business
— learning may involve reappraisal of a 'taken for granted' situation
— learning can happen at a number of different levels
— learning may involve willingness to suspend previous values and attitudes

This intensive work on learning is followed up at various points throughout the year. Within the programme, work on the evaluation of learning centres around secondees' own experience of learning.

More importantly than any content, however, the SFD tutorial team adopt teaching approaches which match with the view of learning discussed in this section. These include the negotiation of many learning tasks within the programme, the attempt to establish a learning climate which is both comfortable and challenging, the use of collaborative group work in a recognition that learners learn well from one another and the exploration of personal learning and experience as a starting point for analysis and discussion of issues (though extension beyond this to the wider referents of theoretical and ideological ideas is essential, too).

It is important that questions of learning arise not only as part of the SFD programme when teachers are out of school, but that these ideas are carried into the heart of school-based commission work. Some commissions have learning overtly on the agenda, but in other cases school tutors have cajoled and encouraged secondees whose commissions had little explicit connection with children's learning towards a sharper, critical consideration of both students' and teachers' learning.

Equal Opportunities

Though the Walton letter (1985) called for changes that would enhance the learning experiences of all students, special mention was made of a large subgroup; the 65 per cent of young people who, even in a time of high youth unemployment, left school at the earliest opportunity. Statistics show that working-class children are over-represented in this group and there is evidence that some ethnic minority subgroups are also disadvantaged by schooling (Eggleston *et al.*, 1986). It has been found, too, that girls and boys traditionally experience differential forms of schooling (Sharpe, 1976; Byrne, 1978; Deem, 1978; etc.) and that girls are less likely than boys to study subjects which give access to higher paid work. An important aspect of school change, therefore, was to rethink the curriculum from the standpoint of these disadvantaged groups.

A concern for equal opportunities lies at the heart of SCI; for example within SFD the team commitment has been made quite explicit. It was decided that equal opportunities (in respect of class, race, gender and disability) was to act as a unifying construct for all activities, rather than as a crucial, but still essentially optional, addition. The SFD team aimed to ensure that this commitment was reflected in the composition of the groups, evident in both the content and processes of the in-service provision and, wherever possible, acted upon at individual and school level. Clearly these represented an ambitious set of targets and not all have been fulfilled. Furthermore, we have found it hard to do more than recognize that the issue of equal opportunities is not merely a matter of improving the situation for those who are most unequal, but that their position is symptomatic of wider issues of power and control both within and between institutions which also require action. The efforts made so far to turn ideological commitments into practice and some of the tensions, challenges and dilemmas that have emerged in the process are discussed below.

The Composition of the Groups

The SFD programme was conceived against a backcloth of LEA cutbacks and rate capping. Harsh economic factors prevailed and, in order for the LEA to balance its books, it was necessary to second highly paid teachers (scale three or above) to the programme and replace them with probationers. This had profound consequences for equality of access for disadvantaged groups. In the case of gender, for instance, the national picture shows that twice the number of men are to be found in these posts as women (DES, 1987). In following the route dictated by financial expediency, the LEA was unwittingly exacerbating the current situation and limiting the career opportunities of a large section of its teaching force.

Black teachers too were disadvantaged. Sheffield LEA employs few black teachers in primary and secondary schools. Currently, they represent about 1 per cent of the teaching force. Most are recent recruits and subsequently in lower scale posts. Career development opportunities are of prime importance to this group of teachers if they are to attain influential positions in the schooling system in order to initiate curriculum change from the inside.

In response to these findings, the initial secondment intentions were modified and some scale one and two teachers brought into the programme. But even so, ninety-eight men as against fifty-three women constituted the first cohort of secondary secondees and only one black teacher was seconded. Thus in the first and largest phase of the SFD programme, the first principle of equal opportunities was effectively breached. Since then, and under different funding arrangements, the situation has improved somewhat. In subsequent years, male secondary teachers (who in Sheffield represent about 54 per cent of the full-time teaching force) received about 60 per cent of the full-time secondments, though a predominance of women from the primary sector created a balance across the programme as a whole. Two other black teachers have been seconded.

By contrast, women have been well-represented within the tutorial team since its inception and this year a black tutor has joined the previously all-white team. Commitment to – and involvement in – the pursuit of equal opportunities is strong within the team. The three part-time tutors spend the rest of their time engaged in advisory work in this field, whilst several of the full-time tutors have experience of researching and writing on race, gender and special needs issues.

The Content and Processes of the In-Service Provision

It is not surprising, then, that the discussion of equal opportunities has formed a substantial part of the formal agenda of the SFD programme. The issues of gender, race and disability have all been explored, and attention has been paid to class through an exploration of power relationships within groups. As well as these sessions, which were primarily designed to raise issues and heighten awareness, an attempt has been made to permeate equal opportunity questions and considerations into all other areas of study. For example, the work on assessment has included an exploration of the possibility of class, race and gender bias; and equal opportunity issues have been considered within the remit of community education. An attempt has also been made to manage the programme in ways which are recognized as being 'friendly' to women. This means that rather than presenting secondees with packages of expertly defined professional knowledge through the vehicle of lectures and seminars, the emphasis has been on learning through group interaction in which value has been placed on personal experience, expressing feelings and the development of peer support. Ongoing evaluation (Polytechnic, 1987) suggests that both male and female secondees have appreciated the secure, supportive climate generated by this way of working. At the same time, we recognize the need to find ways to extend personal experience and to introduce alternative perspectives which do not jeopardise this more equitable way of working.

The SFD team also attempts to work in ways which are congruent with its espoused commitment to equal opportunities. This has been challenging and, at times, problematical. The team has striven to develop collaborative strategies in which equal value has been attributed to each member and decisions have been arrived at democratically. It has sought to eschew the power games observed – and no doubt participated in – in previous institutions. We would suggest that such transitions are not easy to make, and though at times the team may have failed to model the practices it has advocated, this remains a central imperative of its work.

The Impact of the Work on Equal Opportunities on Schooling

To what extent has the in-service work in this area permeated school commissions and resulted in changes in schools? We know that such change is not likely to be quick or easy to achieve, depending as it does on changes in teachers' deep-seated attitudes and beliefs and on the wide-scale acceptance of a new educational pedagogy which may openly challenge previous learning. In the case of special needs, for example, teacher training in the 1960s and '70s is likely to have presented a deficit model of working-class children which suggested that 'school failure' was attributable to home circumstances, rather than weaknesses in curricular provision or the impact of wider social, political or economic circumstances. Nor do we underestimate the disequilibrium experienced by some individuals as they seriously confront issues of race and gender for the first time and the possible impact of this on their relationships both in and out of school. We believe that in-service must seek to bring about this level of personal learning, but also that it must go beyond its influence on the individual if it is to prove a potent force for change in schools.

Evidence from evaluation exercises (Polytechnic, 1986/7) suggests that the work presented through the formal agenda of the SFD programme has had an impact on secondees' thinking. Raised levels of awareness and a keenness to explore different ways of working in schools have been commonly reported. The interest and support of SFD secondees has also given impetus to the work already started by advisory staff, and both tutors and secondees have been involved in establishing working parties and in planning and facilitating curriculum days in schools which focus on equal opportunity issues. Co-ordinators with responsibility for equal opportunities have been appointed in some secondary schools. Equal opportunities has provided the specific focus for a number of commissions. For instance, one school commissioned a secondment for the development of a language awareness course which capitalized on the fact that students brought a number of mother tongue languages into school. Other secondments have focused on gender issues in the curriculum, for example one secondee investigated girl-friendly approaches to learning in technology. Other commissions, not centrally targeting equal opportunities issues, have developed in ways which take them into account. For example, one outcome of work on curricular continuity in an all-white nursery school has been the development of links with a nursery in a multi-ethnic area. Special needs, gender and race questions have all influenced the development of methods of recording achievement (particularly personal and social achievement) as part of assessment commissions.

Integrating Inset

Work under SCI reflects the growing recognition that effective INSET must seek to respond to the agendas set by schools. The recognition that schools have different 'needs' and therefore different priorities for development is embodied in the concept of school review and school self-evaluation. Such practices are now commonplace in some schools and across some authorities (see, for example, Clift *et al.* 1987; Hargreaves, 1983; Rodger and Richardson, 1985), though they are unlikely to have permeated the whole system. A logical outcome of such processes is the development and implementation of tailor-made school-based and school-managed INSET. SCI fits readily within this paradigm of school-initiated and school-focused change though, unlike some other initiatives, it operates within prescribed national and local guidelines. It is also distinguishable as an authority-wide initiative inspired by an LEA.

SCI celebrates a model of curriculum development which sees the teacher as the main focus of activity. Again this is nothing new. Curriculum developers influenced by the work of Stenhouse (1975) placed teacher professional development at the heart of that process. Perhaps where SCI has started to break new ground is in the recognition of the importance of the context of change – that of the whole school. We would not claim to have done much more than begin to understand the dynamics and complexities of the whole process of change, but the approach to INSET advocated by SCI recognizes that curriculum development can be achieved only by working concurrently on staff development and institutional change in which, as Leamish (1988, p. 342) states, the three exist in a 'dynamic, holistic inter-relationship'.

The Question of 'Needs'

SCI's attempt to develop in-service work which acknowledges, and begins to cater for, individual teacher and contextual differences has been reflected as much through course processes, which seek to value and extend teachers' expertise and experience, as through programme content. For example, personal shared reflection, never context free, provides the starting point for the exploration of many issues. We have not, however, made a straightforward shift from agendas set, as in traditional INSET, by course providers to those set wholly by schools or teachers on the basis of their perceived 'needs'. Rather, we have considered the notion of 'needs' as being problematical and have tried to address important questions around the identification of 'needs'. Who defines them, for example, and by what process? In the case of two of the projects within SCI, the direction for change – the 'needs' which schools should attend to – were clearly indicated by the CEO. The Sheffield RAE development asked schools to consider the role of assessment in pupils' learning and its impact on their experience of schooling. Within SFD, too, schools were expected to focus on questions of learning, assessment, equal opportunities, and so on. However, within these parameters schools were asked to identify their own priorities for change. We recognize that this is by no means a straightforward business. Despite the growing advocacy of school evaluation, it cannot be assumed that headteachers and their staffs are well practised in this process of review and curricular planning. Even if they were, we would be concerned if it were being accepted too uncritically, for in our view it assumes a rationality which rarely exists in practice. We perceive change as a less predictable, more problematical process than a simple linear model of change suggests and one which is deeply embedded in the organizational and micropolitical structures of the school.

We also feel that there is a danger that schools working in a 'closed' environment might become parochial in their thinking and develop somewhat idiosyncratic programmes of change. This is a charge that has been levelled at schools engaged in school-based developments (Hargreaves, 1982). To counteract this and to ensure that the priorities identified both locally and nationally are attended to, school-based developments within SFD are set within a centrally directed programme. Within this, key issues (learning, assessment, community education, etc.) are addressed. More recently national developments initiated through the Educational Reform Act have figured prominently on this agenda.

Secondees are encouraged to make connections between the general and theoretical issues raised and practices in their own schools. They are also asked to relate the issues to their own school commissions, so that, for instance, questions of gender have impact on commissions focusing on information technology, languages, mathematics, science etc. The secondees' accounts in Chapter 4 of this volume illustrate the way that aspects of the programme have influenced the development of their commissions. In other parts of the programme, secondees' concerns are taken as the starting point. This is so during tutorial work and also in the groups that are constituted to support secondees working on similar commissions, though here too tutors adopt a proactive role to ensure that crucial theoretical and ideological issues are being addressed. In sum, the provision aims to balance a number of features which at first sight may appear contradictory. It seeks to respond to individual 'needs' within a well-defined framework and to offer a secure, but still challenging, environment in which learning can take place.

The Context of Change: the Whole School

However, in-service work undertaken with individual teachers of whatever quality is in itself no guarantee of change in school. In a discussion of the relative failure of most types of in-service to bring about 'school improvement', Reid *et al.* (1987) conclude that the key to this lack of effectiveness lies in the providers' decisions to identify individual teachers instead of schools as the targets for development.

Whilst engagement in academic, research and practical pedagogic activity may have a profound effect on the development of the individual's professional thinking and result in personal growth, it may be hard to act upon. Changes are most likely to occur within the individual's immediate sphere of influence, usually the teacher's own classroom. This may result in a pattern of teacher development in which theory-making and theory-testing are essentially private activities. In attempting to break this circle, Hoyle (1983) argues that individuals are likely to encounter formidable barriers to change if the proposed innovation challenges the predominant value system, norms, traditional structures or established roles within the school. Reid *et al.* (1987) contend that individual teachers seeking to improve practices through programmes of school-based research are as likely to come up against these barriers as any others. Holly (1987, p. 212) attributes the failure of this type of work to generate 'staff-based enquiry, staff development and the collegial development of the whole curriculum' to its conception, for in starting with the concerns of the individual teacher and trying to work outwards it is designed to solve 'teacher problems' rather than 'school problems'.

It is clear from the account in Chapter 1 that there was considerable impetus for 'change' within Sheffield. Both the need for change and the general direction indicated by the CEO were widely, and in some cases uncritically, accepted. However, a favourable climate is not in itself enough. To accept that there is a need to do more than tinker with the more superficial aspects of an organization is one thing: to examine and challenge the taken-for-granted assumptions that underpin them is much more difficult (Handy, 1976; Schein, 1985; Weick, 1983). It is the invisible tacit features of the culture of an organization which frequently remain so resistant to change. It is difficult, for example, for more than superficial changes to take place in individual classrooms if the surrounding structure and value system remains untouched. As one seconded teacher explained:-

> I knew people were very subject-based and tended to stay in their own departments. Stepping back you could see that the structure of the school forced that. Well some people would have done that anyway, but the structure reinforced it.
>
> Aspinwall, 1987

The way in which a school organization is structured is a reflection of its culture, but although culture and structure are connected, the connection may not always be predictable. For example, a clearly defined structure may be a device through which a headteacher exercises power and control and limits development, whilst in a different culture, a similar structure may be the means through which new ideas can be disseminated easily and thus shared. It has been interesting to note that within SCI the same action has been interpreted differently in different schools. For instance, in some schools the secondment of a deputy head has been regarded as an indication of a willingness amongst senior management to change the status quo, whilst in others it has been regarded as a sign that the headteacher intends to remain in control.

That SCI is directed to finding solutions to school – and not individual teacher–concerns is clearly signalled by aspects of the in-service provision. School tutors, for example, do not remain on the sidelines, but go into schools to work with secondees. The process of negotiating access to, and building relationships with, 'significant others' at all levels within a school's organization provides an excellent opportunity to learn what it means to be part of 'this' organization, and to make explicit at least some of the unexamined assumptions under-pinning practice. From the outset within SFD, the school – as well as the individual teacher–is targeted as the focus for development. Emphasis is put on whole school issues, on staff involvement in identifying the priorities for action and in charting the course of the development. The intention is for the school commission to become the vehicle for an on-going process of staff and institutional development as teachers debate a range of curricular issues which then influence the policies and practices in the school. At the same time, we know (Aspinwall, 1989) that nothing is lost in terms of the personal/profes-sional development of the seconded teacher which arises as a natural consequence of the year's work.

The Role of the Secondee

This way of working has obvious implications for the role of the secondees who need to be clear about their tasks and prepared by their own in-service experiences to capitalize upon the opportunities pre-sented to work with their colleagues in school. Discussion about the secondee role forms part of the induction period of the programme, and any myths that they should act as 'hero(ine) innovators' (Georgiades and Phillimore, 1975) are quickly dispelled. Rather, they are encouraged to perceive themselves as enablers working to empower other teachers to bring about change. The role of the seconded teacher is a demanding one and, in many cases, quite different from anything previously experienced. Secondees are encouraged to develop the skills of working in participative ways and to develop effective communication, counselling and facilitation skills. Secondees are also encouraged to perceive the change process from the viewpoint of other members of staff, to understand the micro-politics of change, and to develop their own theories about their organizations as they examine taken-for-granted assumptions about them. There is evidence, too, of some 'results' in terms of changed practice. Some examples of this imply a reassessment of the school's organizational culture: approaches to staff meetings, with group work (an unheard of organizational structure for most schools) leading to more democratic participation in debate by a larger proportion of teachers. In some cases, this has been a striking development. One teacher with eight years service in a school, reported having spoken in a staff meeting for the first time. The response from other teachers indicated that this was by no means a unique occurrence (Aspinwall, 1987). Obviously there are differences in the ease with which secondees adopt the challenging role advocated by SFD, and this has been found to be one factor which distinguishes developments perceived as being 'successful' from those that are perceived as being less so (Aspinwall, 1988).

To Conclude:

The in-service provision developed to support school-based work within SFD has a number of features which we feel distinguish it from other forms of INSET and which has implications for the experience of the secondees. It is planned on the assumption that seconded teachers will work with – and on behalf of – their colleagues on whole school issues and that the commissions will be geared to the perceived 'needs' of the school within the context of local and national priorities. It is designed, therefore, to equip secondees to make informed decisions about what to change, to take on an in-service staff development role in their own schools, to understand more about institutional management and change and to learn how to evaluate the change programmes that they put into action. We also believe that engagement in this process is likely to bring about deep rooted personal change and promote the professional development of individual secondees.

It is also important to recognize that thinking about managing change within organizations in this way is also a learning experience for tutors. As well as 'acting' within this arena, we too must reflect, read, rethink and be prepared to question our own assumptions. In this area, as in any other, we can only 'teach' what we ourselves need to learn.

The Principles Reflected in Practice: One Example

In the final part of this chapter, we illustrate the way in which the three principles outlined above are reflected in school-based work. This example is taken from the SFS programme.

The brief for the team of five seconded teachers was to investigate classroom interaction, with a view to improving practice, a brief that was both broad and potentially threatening to teachers. With the support of the school tutor, a pattern of enquiry emerged which involved secondees working with colleagues rather than making observations and judgments on them. Significantly, the 'problems' and 'needs' were identified by the practising teachers themselves, not by the secondees or the senior management team of the school. A sketch of one of the several enquiries illustrates the approach.

A mathematics teacher, a senior member of staff but not head of department, requested help with his attempts to introduce investigational approaches into his teaching, a new requirement within GCSE. This teacher had never worked in this way before and, like the majority of maths teachers at the time, lacked the necessary skills and confidence. Two of the seconded teachers agreed to observe all the maths lessons taught to one group of fourth year students for a term. The group was engaged in an investigational project for GCSE. Before starting, the maths teacher and the secondees negotiated a written 'contract', which specified what each was going to do and not do. They decided together that the secondees would adopt different roles. One person took the fairly traditional research role of non-participant general observer and the other seconded teacher became a student for the term, doing all the work required by the students in and out of the classroom. As it happened, this 'student' observer regarded himself as mathematically incompetent (he had failed 'O' level mathematics) and so found it quite easy to respond as a student. Very soon this teacher was accepted by the other students as one of their number, so that he could represent not only his own experience of the learning but those of at least some of his fellow students with whom he talked.

Every week the three teachers met to discuss the progress of the learning within the project, each representing the perspectives of teacher, student and observer. The three found these sharing sessions invaluable – each brought fresh and unanticipated insights to the others, insights which changed practice as the enquiry was taking place. For example, the observer pointed out that a few mathematically able boys were dominating proceedings at the start of the project. The teacher was unaware of this and took steps to bring the girls into practical and discussion work to remedy the imbalance. This observation which pointed up an unintended differentiated attitude towards boys' and girls' learning in mathematics was one of several 'equal opportunities' issues which arose. From the student observer, the teacher learnt of the frustrations and difficulties as well as the enjoyment experienced by the students; as well he got some simple, practical feedback on such as lesson organization, and the comprehensibility of his instructions.

Other teachers in the school worked with secondees in a similar way. For example, design and art teachers were experimenting with an integrated approach in the second year and invited secondees to investigate this development with them. One interesting outcome from this enquiry was the introduction of student evaluation of the learning which took place, an innovation which the art and design staff admitted they would not have thought of without the collaborative support of the secondees.

The written reports which emerged from the several co-investigations of classroom practice were all confidential to the teachers concerned. This arrangement had the full support of the headteacher and senior management team, a demonstration of a trusting approach by management, with real responsibility devolved to classroom teachers. It did not mean, however, that the 'lessons learnt' remained the exclusive property of the participants; on the contrary, many of the insights and conclusions were disseminated beyond the school as well as within it. The mathematics teacher, for example, not only took some in-service responsibility for working with departmental colleagues on investigational approaches but gave a presentation on the subject to the city's heads of mathematics at the Polytechnic.

The improvements in practice which emerged had a positive influence not only on the students but on teachers' understandings of learning and evaluation processes. They experienced the value of an open, investigative approach to classroom practice, with learning viewed as both problematic and a proper subject for reflection. The secondees concluded that the approach they had taken provided an excellent opportunity to develop teachers' practices in the classroom and that there was a detectable shift of emphasis towards a consideration of how students best learn.

The example illustrates how school-focused work under SCI has both been guided by and reflects the three principles outlined in this chapter: the need to set questions of learning firmly in the centre of the curricular stage; the centrality of equality of opportunity; the close interrelationship between staff development and the development of curricula and the institution as well as individual teachers and the importance of a school context and management team sympathetic to change.

References

ARMSTRONG, M. (1980) *Closely Observed Children*, London, Writers' and Readers' Co-operative.

ASPINWALL, K. (1987) *A Climate for Change: A Report on the First Year of Sheffield's School Focused Secondment Initiative*, City of Sheffield Education Department (mimeographed).

ASPINWALL, K. (1988) *Curriculum Development Initiatives: Some Factors Affecting Successful Outcomes*, City of Sheffield Education Department (mimeographed).

ASPINWALL, K. (1989) 'A Bit of the Sun: Teacher Development through an LEA Initiative' in Woods, P. (Ed.) *Working for Teacher Development*, Dereham, Peter Francis, pp. 118–35.

AUSUBEL, D., NOVAK, J.D. and HANESIAN, H. (1978) *Educational Psychology: A Cognitive View*, London, Holt, Rinehart and Winston.

BROWN, P. and ASHTON, D.N. (Eds) (1987) *Education, Unemployment and Labour Markets*, Lewes, Falmer Press.

BRUNER, J.S. (1966) *Towards a Theory of Instruction*, Cambridge Massachusetts, Harvard University Press.

BYRNE, E. (1978) *Women and Education*, London, Tavistock Publications.

CLIFT, P.S., NUTTALL, D.L. and MCCORMICK, R. (1987) *Studies in School Self-evaluation*, Lewes, Falmer Press.

CLOUGH, E., CLOUGH, P. and NIXON, J. (Eds) (1989) *The New Learning: Contexts and Futures for Curriculum Reform*, London, Macmillan.

DEEM, R. (1978) *Women and Schooling*, London, Routledge and Kegan Paul.

DEPARTMENT OF EDUCATION AND SCIENCE (1987) *Statistics of Education: Teachers in Service England and Wales*, 1985, London, HMSO.

DONALDSON, M. (1978) *Children's Minds*, London, Fontana/Collins.

DRIVER, R. (1983) *The Pupil as Scientist?*, Milton Keynes, Open University Press.

EASEN, P. (1985) *Making School-Centred INSET Work*, Milton Keynes, Open University (in association with Croom Helm).

EGGLESTON, J., DUNN, D., ANJALI, M. and WRIGHT, C. (1986) *Education for Some*, Stoke-on-Trent, Trentham Books.
FERGUSON, M. (1982) *The Aquarian Conspiracy*, London, Granada.
FREIRE, P. (1972) *Pedagogy of the Oppressed*, London, Sheed and Ward.
GEORGIADES, N.J., and PHILLIMORE, L. (1975) 'The Myth of the Hero-innovator and Alternative Strategies for Organisational Change' in Keirman, C.C. and Woodford, F.P. (Eds) *Behaviour Modification with the Severely Retarded*, North Holland, Elsevier Excerpta Medica, pp. 313–19.
HANDY, C. (1976) *Understanding Organisations*, Harmondsworth, Penguin.
HARGREAVES, A. (1982) 'The Rhetoric of School-Centred Innovation', *Curriculum Studies*, 14, 3, pp. 251–66.
HARGREAVES, A. (1986) 'Record Breakers?' in Broadfoot, P. (Ed) *Profiles and Records of Achievement, A Review of Issues and Practice*, London, Holt, Reinhart and Winston, pp. 203–27.
HARGREAVES, D.H. (1983) 'School self-evaluation', *Inspection and Advice*, 19, Autumn.
HOLLY, P. (1987) 'Making it count: Evaluation for the developing primary school' in Southworth, G. (Ed.) *Readings in Primary School Management*, Lewes, Falmer Press, pp. 200–35.
HOYLE, E. (1983) 'Computers and Education: a solution in search of a problem?' in Megarry, J. (Ed.) *Computers and Education*, London, Kogan Page.
HUGHES, M. (1986) *Children and Number: Difficulties in Learning Mathematics*, Oxford, Basil Blackwell.
HUNT, J. and HITCHIN, P. (1985) *Projects*, London, Framework Press.
KELLY, G. (1955) *The Psychology of Personal Constructs*, New York, W.W. Norton.
LEAMISH, P. (1988) 'Power, control and the praxis orientation to school-based programme development', *Studies in Educational Evaluation*, 14, 3, pp. 341–59.
MASLOW, A.H. (1968) *Towards a Psychology of Being*, New York, Van Nostrand-Reinhold Co.
PIAGET, J. and INHELDER, B. (1973) *The Psychology of the Child*, London, Routledge and Kegan Paul.
POLYTECHNIC (1986) *Evaluation of Gender Day*, Sheffield City Polytechnic (mimeographed).
POLYTECHNIC (1987) *Evaluation of the Polytechnic Course 1986/7: Some Issues Arising*, Sheffield City Polytechnic, (mimeographed).
REID, K., HOPKINS, D. and HOLLY, P. (1987) *Towards the Effective School*, Oxford, Blackwell.
RODGER, I.A. and RICHARDSON, J.A.S. (1985) *Self-evaluation for Primary Schools*, London, Hodder and Stoughton.
ROGERS, C. (1969) *Freedom to Learn*, Columbus (Ohio), Charles Merrill.
ROWLAND, S. (1984) *The Enquiring Classroom: An Approach to Understanding Children's Learning*, Lewes, Falmer Press.
SCHEIN, E.H. (1985) *Organisational Culture and Leadership*, San Francisco/London, Jossey-Bass.
SHARPE, S. (1976) *Just Like a Girl*, Harmondsworth, Penguin.

STENHOUSE, L. (1975) *An Introduction to Curriculum Research and Development*, London, Heinemann.

STRONACH, I. (1988) 'A critique of the "new assessment": from carnival to currency?' in Simons, H. and Elliott, J. (Eds) *Teacher Appraisal and Pupil Assessment*, Milton Keynes, Open University Press.

WALTON, W.S. (1985) *The Future of Sheffield's Secondary Schools*, Chief Education Officer's letter to Secondary Schools, 17 December, 1985, City of Sheffield Education Department (mimeographed).

WEICK, K.A. (1983) 'Organisational communication – towards a research agenda' in Putnam, L. and Pacanowski, M. (Eds) *Communications in Organisations*, London, Sage, pp. 13–29.

3
From Structure to Practice

Douglas Finlayson, Jeanie Hedge, Colin Martin, Daryl Agnew and Carole Goodwin

In this chapter, three discrete accounts describe something of the work of the main components of SCI – the Management Support Team, the Curriculum and Assessment Resource and the School-focused Development Programme.

The Management Support Team

Douglas Finlayson

The work of the Sheffield Management Support Team (MST) is based on the assumption expressed by Greenfield (1988 p. 132) that 'it is people who are responsible for organizations and people who change them.'

The people who are the concern of the MST are those with formal managerial responsibility in the schools – the headteachers, deputy headteachers, and senior teachers. In relation to them, the MST has not sought to promote any specific changes; rather it has offered support to those with managerial responsibilities in schools in order that they can deal more effectively with demands placed upon them, whether these come from national or local sources, from within their own schools, or from within themselves. This distinction between advocacy and support is basic to an understanding of the work of the MST.

The work of the MST exemplifies a particular kind of learning process. In that process, participants work collaboratively to create and maintain a supportive environment within which they seek to facilitate their own professional development. It is this collaborative process which the MST is advocating. In particular, the MST has sought to enable those with managerial responsibilities to become more aware of the assumptions and largely unconscious patterns of action which constitute their professional practice in schools. By so doing, it is intended that participants in the MST's activities should develop greater insight into their present situations, acquire a greater and more flexible repertoire of possible ways of acting, and have some degree of choice in what they do rather than exercise their authority in an accepting, habitualized and unquestioning way.

By taking as its starting point the issues and concerns of those with managerial responsibility in schools, the work of MST can be seen to be a form of in-service support which, in fact, integrates various forms and levels of development, be they related to the staff as a whole, the curriculum of the school, the school as an organization or of the person with managerial responsibility. As will be demonstrated it is in the last of these areas, concerned with the development of self-managing individuals, that the work of the MST has been focused under the guidance of the author, an independent consultant with a strong belief in the effectiveness of reflection-inspired personal and professional learning.

The nature of the self-managing individual has been clearly described by Lawrence (1979 p. 235)

> The self-managing individual is refusing to allow cultural assumptions to remain untested and he is disentangling the cobweb of myths and mysteries of our social institutions. He has to differentiate what is conventionally agreed to be reality and what is reality for him. Thus, whereas it is widely accepted that the search for scientific objectivity requires the individual to suppress subjective judgment, we would turn the proposition on its head and postulate that objectivity is essentially the clarification of one's own subjectivity.
>
> But as he examines more closely what is inside and what is outside and tries to regulate the boundary between them, the individual is confronting those very cultural forms hitherto taken for granted, that provide the defensive structures and thus confronting his own primitive inner needs that these structures satisfy. In giving up an external definition of 'reality' and substituting his own, he is therefore giving up elements of certainty and security and substituting uncertainty and insecurity.

Our argument is that the resultant disorder and chaos are the necessary risks and costs of undertaking change. Social change inescapably starts with self.

The 'Image Days' Workshop

In an endeavour to help headteachers to clarify their thoughts and feelings about what it was like for them to be headteachers in Sheffield in 1989, an initial series of workshops was organized for as many of the heads of schools in Sheffield as wished to attend. An open invitation was sent to schools in all the sectors of the authority – nursery, infant, junior, secondary and special – and 170 out of a total of 250 head-teachers chose to come. Four groups of around forty headteachers met for a day. Most of the work during the day was done in small groups of eight to ten, each facilitated by a member of the team which had planned the workshop.

In each of the workshops, the participants were invited to create images of how they saw themselves in the role of headteacher in their school, to share their images and to identify some of the reasons why they perceived themselves in that manner. Imaging was chosen as the initial activity of the workshops because images are more than embellishments to thought: they imply a way of seeing the world and oneself in relation to it. In many instances they can provide insights into the 'explanation' for the actions of those who have such images, and serve as an eye to the inner thoughts and feelings associated with those actions.

The range of images produced in each of the workshops was wide but similar themes emerged. Most of the heads saw themselves as being the focus of unrealistically heavy and often contradictory expectations. They conveyed this through the imagery of juggling balls, spinning plates on poles, climbing mountains or walking tight-ropes. The latter two images, together with those of vortices, torpedoes, a lion in a cage struggling to escape, and a boiling cauldron, reflect not only the difficulties they experienced in performing their role but also the high risks associated with it. The risk of error they saw as having serious consequences for themselves and their schools.

Many of them saw themselves as lonely figures, carrying their burden of responsibility alone. The heavy emotional cost to those who saw themselves in this way was reflected in the tears which featured in some of their pictures, and the more common theme portrayed by the large confident smile masking the reality of their inner world, symbolized by a stifled cry of 'Help!' Another image in the same vein was of a sponge soaking up the demands of others and the associated question, 'But to whom can I unload what I have absorbed?'.

All their images of the DES indicated that it was perceived as a source of threat and danger. It was variously portrayed as a gale–force wind, as a bird of prey with blood dripping from its beak, as a jackboot about to crush people underfoot, and as the shark–infested waters surrounding a ship. In discussing these images, powerful feelings were expressed. Most of the headteachers felt angry at the volume of the DES legislation which they saw as the reason for much of the pressure they experienced. Many of them thought that the nature of the legislation also rendered them more vulnerable because it increased their responsibility and formal power, and at the same time, served to inhibit their ability to manage their schools in a collaborative manner. They saw this as a continual drain on their professional energies.

The LEA did not feature significantly in their imagery, perhaps because they were able to articulate their immediate experiences in relation to it very clearly and with much humour. They felt resentment at the many difficulties they experienced in communicating with 'the LEA' and their perceived inability to share their concerns with responsible officials. They saw these difficulties in communication as limiting their entry to an important bank of resources to which they wanted easier access.

Positive feelings were expressed by some heads about the solace of being able to go into a classroom to work with children and about the importance they attached to the personal and professional support which they received from the teachers on their staff. Their most positive feelings were expressed about the help and support which many of them gave and at the same time received from their fellow–heads. In this connection, the importance of the informal networks of headteachers which exist within the authority and which have grown up over the years as a result of contacts established in a variety of ways was acknowledged.

The feelings which characterized the final session in all the workshops were positive and there was evidence of a variety of outcomes resulting from the workshops. Many of the heads were able to achieve a personal synthesis of their own experience. By sharing it and relating it to the experience of other heads they secured validation of their personal knowledge and by the end of the day had worked through negative feelings and taken decisions which were to have useful outcomes for the authority and themselves.

They requested that the importance of support groups for heads be recognised and pointed out that the most convincing way in which they could be legitimated would be for the authority to provide resources to enable those headteachers who wanted to attend such groups to do so. They also suggested that it would be useful to have a Handbook of Guidance for headteachers giving information about responsibilities and contact points within the authority and that there should be designated heads to whom any head could talk urgently and who would be available to visit schools if invited. All these requests relate to the provision of resources designed to support headteachers as individuals in the general exercise of their responsibilities, rather than in the performance of any specific aspect of their role.

These requests were in line with the conclusions of various headteacher working groups (see Morton and Evans, 1987) which had emphasized that heads themselves should play the key role in the support and development of their colleagues, and had recommended that every headteacher should have the opportunity to belong to a support group made up of his or her peers. The authority has agreed to provide resources for this step to take place: the equivalent of two headteachers should be seconded each year to form the core of the Management Support Team. Since September 1988, the team has consisted of six headteachers drawn from all sectors of education, who work with the author's help as independent consultant. At present some of the heads are seconded on a full-time and others on a part-time basis: it is not yet clear what the most appropriate arrangement should be. They have been involved in a range of activities, but only their work with support groups will be described here.

The informal support groups within the authority have generally been regarded as serving a useful purpose for headteachers. Perhaps for this reason, it was assumed that the meaning of the term 'support' is likely to be generally understood by everyone. A similar assumption has pervaded the literature dealing with this notion and it is only recently that attempts have been made to understand the complexity of this concept. The latter part of this section will give an indication of how the MST has worked and of some of the outcomes associated with its work.

Self-Managing Support Groups

Two support groups to encourage headteachers to manage themselves more effectively in their role have been established for those who wished to join such a group. These groups have a particular way of working which distinguishes them from other support groups already existing within the authority. The new support groups have between ten and twelve members. Their agenda is set by the members themselves and the focus is primarily on the personal and social processes which are on going within the group. At the moment, each group is facilitated by the author but in order to extend these opportunities to more headteachers, a training group which includes the heads seconded to the MST and several other SCI tutors has been set up. It is also anticipated that, in time, the members of those groups will assume more autonomy and become more effective in supporting each other.

At the time of writing, each of the support groups has met for three whole day sessions. Both groups started off by exploring the meaning of the notion of support using their own experience of it – the benefits and risks associated with the process, and identifying the behavioural guidelines which are conducive to its creation and development. These guidelines have become the normative bases or ground rules on which the groups now operate. The first group went on to look at how they might support each other. This led them to want to explore the manner and extent to which they are responsible for their own feelings of guilt and inadequacy. The second group has begun to examine the processes of negotiation and the skills of active listening which are an essential part of that process.

The confidentiality of the sessions, the action-based nature of the learning and the dynamic nature of the interactions that constitute the group process of the support groups, posed problems about the kind of illustrative material which it would be useful to provide. In the end, I decided that the words of the participants themselves would be the best medium to convey something of their experience of working in the groups. Accordingly, I asked a few of them to write a brief account of their experience. They did not find this an easy task: one of the contributors estimated that it took him nearly eight hours to write a page and a half because of the difficulty of finding the right words to articulate his experience!

This participant begins his account by confirming the central importance of his own personal development in the learning process when he says this about his experience:

I have learned so much of value. Of paramount importance is the discovery that I cannot separate personal and professional development. When I reflect on what I have learned I relate it to both myself as a person and to how I use it personally and professionally. I can say of all the learnings that they derive from me as a person and find application in me as a person and me in a role: nothing I have learned has derived from me in role. My role has given rise to reflections and explorations, but these have always led me to discoveries about myself as a person... Through these groups I encountered and faced for the first time some things about myself which I had previously failed to learn and act upon. These had a very paradoxical nature of them; they came in a real sense with the power of revelations but at the same time with a familiarity that placed them not only firmly in me but also suggested an awareness I had successfully suppressed.

This process of denial is also recognized by another head who became aware of it in the course of sharing one of her concerns with a partner in the group.

I had taken upon myself the role of, as I saw it, the maintainer of good relations in difficult working conditions at school – the building was undergoing rewiring – keeping everyone operating as normally as possible and with the minimum of disruption to the children's work. The rewiring began during the Autumn half-term holiday. Just before Christmas I contracted a severe sore throat and lost my voice. I declined my doctor's advice to take time off to rest it ... preferring instead to take a course of antibiotics which the doctor reluctantly prescribed as he said they were unlikely to be effective ... After the Christmas holiday ... the rewiring was still continuing. At this time as well, I became increasingly preoccupied and was spending a lot of time (which I begrudged) on another issue concerning the accommodation of the local branch library in our school building. Also my sore throat returned which I blamed on the dust in the school. As I related all this to my partner I became very tearful.

When helped to explore her reaction, this head was able to:

acknowledge feelings which I had not allowed myself to recognize. This was an uncomfortable experience – like having a tooth drawn – but I was very glad I 'stayed with it'. I learned that I was being unfair to myself to put myself under such pressure; that to take time away from the problem situation allows you to return to deal with it more effectively – in fact the problem may be less serious than it first appeared.

She concludes by saying that she no longer feels guilty about needing to take time for herself nor, she hoped, will she let herself think that she is indispensable in any situation.

Another participant confirms the action-based nature of the learning. He writes that for him the most valuable part of the learning situation has been in watching the process of counselling the members of his support group.

I found this even more valuable than trying an exercise with a colleague that I knew and trusted. I feel sure that both ... were needed in order for it to have meaning.

The comment which follows illuminates what the process of counselling meant to this respondent.

I cannot produce an inventory of what I learned.

Then he goes on to say:

On reflecting upon what happened to me I think the process was one in which I opened up to myself. I was able to do this by having time and space to talk, and having someone who really listened to me. It was also vital that the person kept with me, reflected back to me what I had said and invited me to go deeper by asking questions arising from what I had said. Some of these experiences were seemingly simple: a question such as 'Who is doing that to you?' through which I recognized the contradictory expectations I was holding of myself. At other times the process was difficult, even painful. Always though, I knew when I hadn't reached what I wanted to find and I knew when I had reached it.

In order to facilitate the reflective process, sometimes the participants worked in pairs. On one such occasion, the members of the group were exploring the nature of the 'rules' which they imposed upon themselves and endeavouring to come to some conclusion about the rationality of these rules. One headteacher started off with what appeared to be a fairly common and straightforward rule – 'I must improve the organization of my time.' Almost one hour later, and after identifying the nine steps in the hierarchy of rules to which this particular rule belonged, he eventually reached the rule from which most of his organizational problems came. This was, 'I must be what others want me to be.' When he reached this point he rose slowly to his feet, said how difficult the journey had been, but expressed great satisfaction at having got there. He had a new awareness of the manner in which he was creating problems for himself in organizing his work in school and elsewhere.

Even within the short time in which these groups have been running there is evidence of positive outcomes. One head reports a considerable easing of the stress he had been under.

> Many of the stresses I was experiencing have been reduced. I now know more about myself and my responsibility for the situations I am in. I am more aware of the choices I can make and the choices others can make; consequently I am more honest with myself and with others.

Several of the respondents reported that they have become aware of new ways of working with members of their staff and are in the process of developing new skills. One participant reports, for example, in an account written at the beginning of March that:

> I have found myself on three occasions since 1st February trying to talk to people in much the same way as I had seen you talk to members of our support group. On the first occasion it was with a member of staff who seemed to be finding it very difficult to cope because he felt he had to do everything himself, and to do it to an impossibly high standard. He felt it was what people expected of him.

He goes on to say:

> Just yesterday ... at a staff meeting where a working party on staff relationships was reporting, the following statement was made: 'we are constantly being bombarded by new ideas and new demands and seem to spend so much of our time doing a lot of different things – and doing nothing well. All this against a background of hostile public opinion.' The staff spent a lot of time discussing this statement – especially the comment that we did nothing well. I focused discussion on 'who says we do nothing well?' We eventually agreed that, in relation to our school, in the main it was us – we were the people who created those feelings of dissatisfaction. ... We often appeared guilty of setting ourselves impossible demands and targets.

Another comment in a similar vein is:

> I am aware that I listen much more carefully and check that I have heard what people have said to me. I am much more confident about being able to support others for I no longer feel it is my place to solve their problems for them. I now seek to support them as they find their own solutions. This has benefits for me and them.

This respondent also maintains, in line with Lawrence's picture of the self-managed person, that:

> I have been freed of many culturally derived ideas about my job – the myths of headship.

He went on to give a verbal account of an occasion during the previous week. He had been called upon to intervene in a situation where one of his pupils had been accused of stealing a knife. He reported that he no longer felt obliged to play the role of the grand inquisitor or of the ultimate punishing deterrent. Rather did he seek to move the boy from a flagrant denial of his act to an awareness of the basis of his action. This lay in the nature of his relationship with his parents. When this headteacher subsequently interviewed the boy's parents he felt much more confident about talking to them, because he no longer felt afraid of the consequences of departing from the traditional mythical role of headteacher.

Perhaps we can leave the final word about the support groups to this participant. He says:

> I have spent the whole of my working life stressing the importance and value of individuals and the necessity of working from where somebody is and valuing experience. The support group is the first time I have experienced the power of this for myself. I am becoming more comfortable with my feelings and thoughts and have heard some valuable things from myself. Prior to the support group I would not – could not – have written that I need to learn what I have described above, and yet now I cannot imagine being unaware of them.

The climate of such groups is crucial to their success. For the participants to confront themselves in a way which leads them to new insights is demanding, both cognitively and emotionally, and it is important for the facilitator to provide an optimum challenge and at the same time keep the risk involved for the participants within manageable proportions. Maintaining that balance is the essence of support. It does not imply dependency rather does it refer to a process which has as its outcome the development of self-managing respondents.

That the headteachers who have been involved in the groups report some changes in themselves is encouraging as is the fact that most of them continue to have a positive attitude to themselves as learners. But it would be premature to assume that the cognitive, emotional and behavioural changes reported by the headteachers are transferable from the support group to the context of their schools on a scale which might significantly affect the climate and culture of their schools. The extent to which such changes at the level of the organizations for which they are responsible will be influenced by many considerations. Nevertheless, the outcomes which have been reported to date suggest that the concept of support is a useful one for the personal and professional development of headteachers, and a necessary one to complement the advocacy of any significant degree of educational change.

The Curriculum and Assessment Resource

Jeanie Hedge and Colin Martin

In September 1987 nine teachers were seconded with a member of the Advisory Service to the Curriculum and Assessment Resource (CAR) to support schools in developing a Sheffield Record of Achievement and Experience (RAE). We began our work by exploring first the implications of the policy statements from the DES, 1984 and from Sheffield LEA (1987) which suggested something other than a limited view of learning and assessment and second how to translate our thinking into effective work with schools without imposing an LEA prescription.

Background to the Work of CAR

The newly formed Record of Achievement Panel based at CAR began its work with very mixed perceptions of the task and how to set about it. The initial process and reflection which this group of teachers went through is closely linked with the ways in which CAR subsequently developed its work in support of recording achievement in Sheffield secondary schools.

We began by sharing our recent and common experience of

teaching. We were all uneasy with the narrow and prescriptive labelling of children resulting from purely teacher-led assessment and in particular with the heavy emphasis on examination results. We all personally knew of children who left school sadly disadvantaged by a system which did not recognize a student's many and varied talents and attributes other than those credited by the exam. board; a system which recognized only examination success. In thinking through the implications of this for our task of promoting a RAE, we realized the many shortcomings inherent in assessment by objectives and its subsequent recording through teacher-identified criteria. If the RAE was to be a worthwhile enterprise for students and not merely a bureaucratic refinement, a radical shift focusing on a recognition of the value of the individual and her or his personal construct of learning and experience was necessary. This is hardly a revelation for many teachers who often cite examples of pupils with considerable talents or experience which is acquired either outside the curriculum or deemed low status within it. Certainly there is no means of recognizing the student's achievements in the round. The problem focused on the undue value attached to the existing system of assessment, the lack of opportunity to credit anything other than the traditional academic examination performance and crucially the lack of confidence of teachers themselves in positively valuing, promoting and supporting students' involvement in their own learning. The RAE pointed the way to a radical shift in the relationship between teacher and learner since it implied that students took a greater responsibility for their own learning. It was a powerful force for curriculum change.

With this view of student learning as a foundation we considered how best to pursue the task in schools. We considered our own adult learning. We had all been on numerous courses and been at the receiving end of packages designed to bring about substantial change in classroom practice. We began to understand the importance of valuing the individual experience and needs of adult learners as much as that of the students. We recognized the importance of context, climate, relationships, support and challenge in our own learning and the implications of this for our INSET with schools.

Initiatives in schools were very varied and reflected the priorities and styles within each institution. Some schools had begun to develop recording in the upper school and already had a summative record, others had concentrated on the lower school or particular departmental work, others had not yet begun to consider the RAE. Access to schools was very variable, too. Some schools invited CAR personnel in to assist with staff meetings or with Curriculum Days, some departments invited CAR to their meetings, some expressed little interest at all. The LEA allocated members of CAR into the newly developed meetings of clusters of schools which provided us with contact with headteachers. CAR began to establish contacts and build networks across the schools to share, discuss and consult. Such networks extended beyond the secondary sector to include some tertiary colleges and also increasingly some primary schools. Although we perceived our role as centrally committed to formative classroom process we consulted with representatives from industry and commerce as partners in the Sheffield RAE. This consultative way of working became a main feature of the CAR style.

One example of CAR's work: A Cluster Day on RAE

The consortium of schools known as the D/E cluster comprising five secondary schools, two secondary special schools and one tertiary college had already established a group to share experience of RAE. This meeting was attended by senior staff from each of the five comprehensive schools. These schools were very different in their ethos as well as in the RAE developments under way. The two CAR members attached to the formal cluster meeting were invited to join this group and over the next few months we played our part in the meetings. Initially there was suspicion on both sides about our role and purpose in so doing. Were we there to impose an LEA prescription? Did we have a covert purpose which would affect the work in schools? On our part we felt uneasy about what was expected of us both by the schools and by our LEA employers.

This was a valuable period for establishing personal contacts and for acquiring an understanding of the issues and directions relevant to the cluster in the wider LEA context. The CAR members were able to begin to raise some of the issues of RAE from the experience gained through our knowledge of other schools and the national pilot schemes. Around the end of the second term of 1988 each school had made its contribution, the group seemed to have achieved its objectives. The CAR personnel had a different perspective. By then the LEA had decided to use clusters to meet the TVEI-Extension demand for schools to work in consortia and the development of the RAE was an important part of the cluster bid for funding.

The newly introduced curriculum training days were presenting schools with some difficulties in that they required staff with the skills of group facilitation. Few teachers felt confident of their ability to work with their colleagues but schools were looking to DIY. The first venture into cross-cluster support instigated from and by CAR was a day for two colleagues from each of the schools intended to challenge perceptions around facilitation within a supportive framework. We designed a programme for the day which modelled the actual practice and which identified the need for sharing experience, attentive listening, flexibility, which was non-prescriptive and allowed all participants to become involved. We explored a wide range of issues as they were identified by the teachers around the need for genuine collaboration, creating a climate which was open and non-threatening and which helped teachers to build confidence.

It is not at all easy to describe how such a climate is achieved other than to reassert the central importance of recognizing each individual's perception of learning. We felt that it was important to work in this way rather than present ourselves only as RAE experts in order to facilitate a sense of ownership of the issues among teachers. Time spent helping teachers to improve their group facilitation skills was an important part of this process. Members of the group were able to talk about their anxieties in facilitating their colleagues in terms of the expectations they felt others had of them and the difficulties they experienced in trying to bring about curriculum change. They recognized and questioned the place of hierarchy, status and competition in their work.

The success of this first venture led easily into the notion of a cross-cluster Curriculum Day. The importance of establishing the cluster as a community of collaborative institutions was rhetorically cited in the cluster TVEI-E bid. There was recognition at all levels that co-operation across the schools rather than competition between them would benefit both staff and students alike. The demands of government legislation could best be met by joint initiatives and collaborative action.

The cluster D/E RAE group proposed a joint Curriculum Day on RAE and delegated CAR to raise the idea at the meeting of cluster headteachers which by this stage now included two special schools. This we duly did, anticipating that support for the idea would be unproblematic. This was not the case. Some had already planned the use of the training days, some felt the level of staff expertise in group leadership was unavailable. In the event it took some time to reach agreement and even more time to agree the date as being the first day of the January term.

Once mandated the RAE group was enthusiastic about the task and anxious about the potential for very public failure. The logistics of the exercise were daunting since the total teaching staff in the cluster was very large – more than 350 colleagues! More important than the numbers involved was getting the process right. It became clear that CAR had an important role in supporting group and individual morale.

Over the summer the two CAR members thought about what was involved for the whole group in terms of planning, consultation, briefing and evaluation. At the first meeting in September we presented the group with a proposed schedule of targets and points of process for the term. It was received in silence and subsequently ignored. We had broken our own basic ground rule of working with people rather than prescribing for them. Following this salutory experience the task became a genuinely group effort though within the group the CAR members' role differed from that of the school representatives.

The term from September to Christmas was a crucial one. There is no doubt that the scale and high profile of the task was very important in engendering commitment from the group. However, it is important to say that there was an overt and exciting sense of pioneering a new venture based on a collaborative working ethos which the group felt it had already demonstrated. This realization that the model by which the RAE group functioned would be reflected in the process leading up to and including the day itself for our colleagues in school, consolidated our ground rules. The climate generated by the group was of central importance and though this dynamic evolved through the individual members of the group there were also processes consciously initiated by the CAR members and made explicit as groundrules. These involved clarifying that both the task and the responsibilities attached to it were shared by us all from the outset, that though the members of the group had different roles, experience, gender or status this should not disadvantage individuals and that our decisions were reached by discussion and consensus. It was also clear from the outset that the day would require considerable planning time which would have to be found over and above other commitments. In practice we came to be very open and honest about difficulties, both personal and organizational, which we encountered; there was also encouragement and recognition when things went well. In so far as SCI is about preparing schools to meet the challenge of change, the process that this group went through can be seen as being more important than the outcome in terms of RAE.

The composition and size of the group had altered. It had been a group comprising mainly assistant heads. Originally there were very few women. The group now expanded to include the two cluster special schools, the SFD tutors attached to the cluster, a representative from the tertiary college and the Careers Service, and the SCI evaluator. It now numbered eighteen. The consultations with staff in schools along with other aspects of the organization of the day were very onerous and some schools were represented by two or more people. The group had become very mixed. It was no longer dominated by senior staff; there were proportionately many more women. Some schools were more advanced with RAE and some of the newcomers may well have felt they lacked expertise initially but they were welcomed and continued to come to meetings. The sense of belonging was expressed by one member:

> From me who knew nothing about RAE (do I yet?) I now feel PART OF IT ALL – THANKS!

Meetings became less formal in their style in spite of the increasing importance of meticulous organization. People joined in discussion freely without deference to those more senior. Although some group members felt unsupported in their schools, within the group there was no sense of competition or rivalry. The group collaborated, shared its ideas and the jobs.

These views expressed by members of the group as part of the evaluation of their work after the day articulate a feeling most of us do not experience very often in our working lives:

— the group solidarity grew and was a pleasure to be part of.
— the task had its tense moments but the feeling of shared responsibility and effort minimized this.
— very good group to work with. Whenever there was a job there were people offering to do it.

The planning group discussed and concluded that workshops should concentrate on the issues of formative classroom process. The consultations with colleagues in school supported this view. There was a clear demand from staff for workshops addressing recording on a subject basis as well as whole school issues, e.g. the recording of personal qualities, the place of RAE within the pastoral and guidance curriculum, the impact of RAE on learning and an introduction to the principles underlying recording for those staff not previously involved. We set up small groups to draft the programme of the fifty-one workshops and CAR and SFD members provided support in terms of experience of staff development and knowledge of RAE initiatives in other schools. Good clerical support was available through CAR and this proved invaluable for efficient and widespread communications. Supply time available to CAR was used to support a week of workshops which the planning group ran for the school-based facilitators. We did not assume that colleagues could facilitate groups without support. These sessions for facilitators provided the opportunity to discuss, influence and contribute to the workshops, to create or provide materials and to widen the sense of involvement and ownership of the day. We designed evaluation sheets for each session and devised systems for recording the ideas, contacts and problems suggested by our colleagues. Further working groups were set up to plan communications, accommodation, logistics and collate lists of participants and facilitators for the day. We organized time for the planning group to collate and interpret the responses generated by each of the fifty-one workshops after the day and to take stock ourselves.

It was a very large task. One participant commented:

A bit like a wedding – a hell of a lot of planning and over in a flash. Was it worth it? Yes, definitely.

The thorough planning paid off and there were no organizational blunders. As one might anticipate not all the workshops were equally well received by the teachers. The first day back after a short Christmas holiday does not engender widespread enthusiasm. Curriculum Days are still the cause of much strong feeling. The planning group was gratified that the day itself was thought to be worth it.

The wedding is merely the beginning of a marriage. The comments made by teachers from the seven schools have provided valuable indicators for the future. All the groups referred to the management of time and resources to support new approaches to teaching and learning. The implications of RAE for classroom practice in terms of more student-centred and less didactic teaching, with the need for attitudinal change and the development of understanding and skills, pointed up the need for supporting INSET. Ideally, this should be available not only for teachers but also for students, parents and employers. All groups recommended further cross-cluster links particularly for subject areas and valued the sharing of experience and information across the schools as a way of enhancing individual school developments.

Since the Day, the group has met with the headteachers to look to the future. Some cross-cluster development groups are already in existence and more are planned. A cluster newsletter will be published soon to make ideas available and exchange information. CAR will support and co-ordinate these activities. A further consultation with staff is already under way, the heads have supported a second cross-cluster Curriculum Day and CAR will liaise with the schools to agree both the date and content of this day. The new development groups to support TVEI-E work will link with RAE through CAR.

The original purpose of the day was to raise awareness of the RAE issues faced by schools. With CAR's support much more became possible. The conventional response to such a commission would be a programme of expert inputs and seminar discussion, perhaps on a cascade principle. What such training misses out is the sense of personal learning which many teachers experienced and which is so much more likely to lead to changes in actual practice. In addition it is likely that important lessons about the excitement of collaborative activity will transfer to future use of training opportunities. Most of all, many teachers will have tasted the experience of being involved in the consideration of major change in an atmosphere of enthusiasm rather than anxiety:

> — I never thought I'd say this but I'd really miss this group if it folded. I sincerely hope it doesn't!

The School Focused Development Programme: The Core

Daryl Agnew and Carole Goodwin

The out-of-school SFD programme contains a common element for all seconded teachers – the core programme – where themes and ideas which are reflections of local and national priorities are encountered. Secondees work, as well, on commission-related issues – thus, teachers with a brief to work on assessment, for example, meet together with a tutor to share ideas and support. Each member of the tutorial team is allocated a number of schools and these school tutors work with secondees in school teams both in and out of school. The programme also includes an induction programme, a residential experience for all secondees and a number of optional seminars, workshops, visits, etc. The planning of the programme is the responsibility of the tutorial team but help and expertise from many other sources – the advisory and support services, higher education, national projects, and so on – is called upon at various points in the programme.

This account describes the core programme of the secondment year, its rationale, and some responses of the seconded teachers towards it. One secondee's comment sums up what the tutorial team hopes to achieve in this part of the programme:

— Colleagues on the course have made me much more aware of myself as an educator, as being a person involved with teaching children and respecting their views – by listening and commenting during sessions, they provided a slightly different viewpoint which before I had not considered.

The Induction

The core begins with an intensive three week induction period during which teachers work in groups of about twenty-five, together with the three tutors responsible for their schools. One of the main aims of the induction period is to create an effective group in which members will feel safe to explore their previous experience and feelings, so that this group develops into a learning and support group for the whole year. As tutors, we aim to acknowledge the wealth of experience the secondees are bringing with them and to work with them in ways which help them to re-examine their classroom practice and their relationships in school with both pupils and colleagues.

One exercise we regularly use is called a timeline in which secondees (and tutors) map out on paper the key incidents and learning experiences which have helped to shape their thinking as teachers. The timeline is constructed individually at first, then some experiences are shared in pairs and, following that, in groups of four where similarities and differences of choice are discussed. The timelines vary greatly. Some secondees choose very personal events – marriage, births, the death of relatives and close friendships. Others stick to professional experiences – university or college and employment patterns. The aim is not only to encourage the sharing of information in order to develop a viable group, but also to draw out from teachers their *feelings* about education, significant people in their lives and events that have influenced them. We invite them to try to relate this experience to assumptions about the learning of pupils within and outside the classroom.

Clearly it is important to establish groundrules for work of this nature very early on in the induction period. Confidentiality within the group is of great importance when many Sheffield schools, and some individual teachers within them, can easily be identified by others. Allowing everyone within the group the chance to air their views without being 'put-down' by others is another important groundrule to establish. By trying to be hard on issues, but not on people, we consciously encourage the quieter members of the group to offer their views and avoid domination by the vociferous minority. One area of lively debate is the difference in 'airspace' that is taken by male and female members of the group; we find that work in pairs and small groups results in something more equitable. One secondee described her early reactions:

> At the beginning I was extremely cautious about exposing myself – the programme and active learning methods quickly enabled me to be comfortable with small groups. Some of the group may have felt there was too much groupwork but, for myself, and some of the others within the group, it was a necessary development and would have reduced our role within the group if we had not had the time to reflect/expose in a size of group in which we could respond.

The contexts in which teachers are working on their commission – the school climate, traditions and relationships within the staff are also explored. Our contention is that these areas are crucial to an understanding of, and success in, managing the changes which teachers are expected to accomplish in their year's secondment. We invite teachers to 'image' their schools, to draw their schools and themselves in it. The exercise begins individually (frequently with much complaining about the lack of drawing skills!), then the drawings are shared with others in the group. The drawer explains the detail, both thoughts and feelings, of the image. We find that teachers consider themselves, irrespective of their status in the school, to be at times quite powerless in determining change. Feelings are explored and expressed, so that a realistic picture is built up which recognizes both the cognitive and affective areas in working environments and professional lives. This exploration of both opinions and thoughts about our work and commissions, and also our feelings about the school in which we are working, is a crucial part of the whole core programme, as well as of the induction period.

During this three week period individual commissions are also set within a broader educational context. We look at the local projects involved in the Sheffield Curriculum Initiative, the national context of the Education Reform Act and the global context of educational change. Some secondees welcome this widening of their previous experience:

> The support I got from the core programme has been immense. Maybe I am someone who had thought: 'What the hell is student-centred learning' or 'What has anti-racism got to do with all-white schools?' or 'I don't need to worry about local financial management' ... so the particular support that I have got is that the space has been created to air what feels to me to have been a wide range of issues in the course of the day; on any given one there have been literally heaps of ideas surrounding the issue pouring in from all sides.

Others, however, approach the induction period with sceptisim. A number of secondees start at the beginning of the year with considerable reservations about the organized part of the programme; it is sometimes seen as an intrusion on their commission:

> My initial reactions were very mixed. For example, I began the first week expecting to be working on my commission. My reaction was – what was all this about? Why am I doing this? I was rather resentful of 'wasting' time. I enjoyed the activities but I was not involved in their relevance.

This teacher felt that she had a clearly defined task for the year, and wanted to go ahead to pursue it. She saw limited value in what she defined as 'extraneous activities' which took away time from her main task in school. This is a frequently experienced dilemma, which first appears within the induction programme, but also emerges at times during the core programme: the reluctance to acknowledge the relevance of wider educational concerns. As tutors, however, we strongly encourage all secondees to take time within the core programme to develop their commission further. For example, a secondee may have a commission to develop a technology course for the upper school. Although issues of race, gender and special needs may not appear at first sight to be intrinsic to the commission, questions are asked about pupil access to the course, the way in which materials are presented, course content, teaching and learning processes and the attitudes of pupils and teaching staff. It is intended that, through this process of questioning, stepping back from the task and seeking clarification from colleagues, secondees will become better able to refine their original commission.

At the end of the induction period we evaluate the experience for teachers in the groups and try to understand secondees' priorities for work throughout the year. These agendas are then discussed within the team and our own ideas are placed alongside those of secondees. Topics such as staff development, the management of change in school, evaluation, equal opportunities, assessment and learning usually emerge as important, and a core programme is developed around them. After this initial consultation process on topics for the core, the tutorial team takes responsibility for the processes of the core days as well as details of their scheduling.

The Core Programme

This takes place approximately one day every fortnight for the remainder of the academic year. A set of questions underpin the whole programme and provide continuity for the various core inputs. These questions are:

— what personal beliefs do we bring to our understanding of ...... (special needs, community education, etc.)?
— what has shaped and influenced these understandings?
— what other evidence and perspectives do I need to extend my understandings?
— what internal constraints operate against their reformulation?
— what external factors operate against their re-formulation?
— what personal responsibility do I have for this within my own institution?
— what sort of evidence is needed to make the issues accessible to my colleagues?
— how real are the issues outside a teacher professional audience? (e.g. to parents, governors, politicians, etc)
— to what extent can these issues be considered without recourse to their political implications?

These have served best as an 'aide-memoire' for tutors planning different core days. Some of them are clearly reflected in the thinking behind the programme for special needs.

In order to give a flavour of the planning that goes into the programme and its underlying rationale, we will look at a two-day special needs event. The days presented a challenge to our usual charitable notion of special needs on the first day, demonstrating instead an equal opportunities analysis of special needs, where the focus is on rights and access. On the following day the aim was to root these ideas within both the experience of secondees' own commissions, and the present political climate of change. We chose to begin by bringing the special needs issue towards a personal understanding of teachers' own experiences, to take it away from being only about 'them out there'.

The programme looked like this:

Day 1

    * In core groups secondees are asked to reflect on their personal experience of finding difficulties in learning and to share these within the larger group.

    * A values clarification exercise – The Integration Rack (Clough, 1989) in groups of four, secondees look at statements, culled from the research literature on special needs around integration issues, and are invited to discuss these to see whether they can reach agreement. The statements become progressively more controversial.

    * A disabled person from the Forum For People with Disabilities in Sheffield gives a personal view on how disabled people are treated in schools and in society.

    * In core groups, follow-up discussion from earlier talk, with a focus on what action we can take.

Day 2

    * A structured examination of case study material to look at how teachers handle children who show common special needs.

    * Teachers work in commission support groups looking at the implications of some of the ideas which are raised for them as individuals and for their schools.

    * In core groups the implications of the Education Reform Act for children with special needs is examined – two background

papers, one arguing that ERA will benefit special needs children, one that it will make their position in schools more difficult, are presented and used either for discussion or as cameos for role-play.

Much of the first morning is therefore spent engaging with different interpretations of special educational needs in a structured exercise – the Integration Rack – which invites debate around published statements on integration, taking participants through 'weak' interpretations such as 'The purpose of education for all children is the same; the goals are the same. But the help that individual children need in progressing towards them will be different' (DES, 1978) to much more challenging ones such as: 'The concept of special education need is a relative one, the need is seen as the outcome of the interaction between the resources and deficiencies of the child, and the resources and deficiencies of his environment' (Wedell, 1985). The intention is to discover – by exposing tacit personal values to a community of criticism – at what point individuals surrender a committed position to the known realities of school life.

In order to assess the impact of this work on special needs and how it was understood and interpreted by seconded colleagues, we asked an experienced special needs teacher in each group to act both as a participant and observer. We brought these teachers together at the end of the two days and discussed with them the processes involved in the activities and in particular asked whether the ideas presented locked into and challenged secondees' previous experience.
One special needs specialist reported:

> Everyone had obviously taken something very positive away. It ranges from a personal thing that 'I'm going to go back to school to question special needs policy that we have or haven't got' ... to people who want to do personal things in their classrooms .. to people who are going to do things outside school.

Another felt disappointed with the small group discussion following the speaker's contribution:

> Everybody got hung up. We did come up with a few suggestions but it's such a massive problem to overcome in society in general. I don't think they were passing it off, but I don't think they could really see what they, as one person, could do.

As tutors we also learned (again!) of the gap between what we thought we were communicating and what secondees were learning. We expected the greatest challenge to come from reactions to the disabled speaker's strong presentation. In fact, this personal view was accepted. However, secondees perceived problems around the area of their personal power to influence change, particularly where this required a large change in values or attitudes within the school. Evaluation of the days the following week also highlighted, not surprisingly, the wide range of meanings which secondees had derived from the two days. Teachers interviewed one another about their reactions – what they found thought-provoking and what implications had arisen for them as individuals and for their schools.

Some clearly felt powerless to influence the interpretation of special educational needs in their own schools. Others resolved to take up practical questions (such as access for physically disabled students to their schools) the following week! Yet others were alerted to the need to re-examine the readability and design of curricular materials and to re-think the use of support staff within their schools.

Throughout the induction and core programme one of our main aims is to provide a support group for secondees. This is vital since many secondees experience considerable anxiety as a result of pressure from school colleagues to 'deliver' on their commissions. Much in teacher culture is, after all, geared to 'action' at the expense of critical reflection. Therefore, one of the major tasks facing us as tutors is enabling a supportive climate to develop within the core group. However, there is clearly a danger that groups will become too cosy, too inward looking, with people shying away from challenges for fear of upsetting group cohesion. As tutors we try to find ways of stimulating debate and discussion, by introducing materials and ways of working which will provoke controversy and, in so doing, to attempt to maintain the fine balance between support and challenge. This tension is reflected in the following comments:

> Being part of the group has benefited me, I feel, in many ways – the chance to discuss topics about education in an open forum in which people are prepared to listen and either accept your point of view or challenge it critically. This has been very stimulating.

and...

> I believe there has been a good balance between support and challenge. All too often I have carried on in a mode of thinking,

believing it to be correct without critically challenging those points and asking why? Certainly the core has challenged some of these thoughts.

SFD is a non-selective programme – teachers come into it with wide varieties of background and experience. Some secondees come with a well-developed critique of what is happening within schools and classrooms whereas other secondees have given less thought to what might be seen as theoretical concerns in education. For these teachers it is often their colleagues within the group who provide the challenge to thinking. The following quotations from secondees speak for themselves:

— Even where there has been challenge it has been refreshing to feel that it is OK to disagree. People aren't afraid of conflicting views and as you grow to respect other individuals you come to accept some of those challenges and enjoy the fact that they accept some of yours.
— Working with colleagues has been of great importance. The ideas we have bounced off each other have stopped time being wasted, finding out what is available when others can provide it. Many secondees have similar commissions and by working together there has been a lot of cross-fertilization of ideas and clarification of what we are doing. From lots of 'bits', my commission has become more refined, more positive and a much more interesting and exciting process.
— I have been challenged on many occasions in the sense that it has become clear that I am not the most radical person on every issue. Once you accept that you may be somewhere between two other people on an issue, you have to accept that exactly where you are is up for discussion and you have to examine that and perhaps more.

As tutors we are, of course, not able to predict the learning outcomes for secondees – some of them clearly doubt the long-term effects.

I'm not sure that the core days will have a lasting effect on the people involved because time limits have prevented the group from exploring particular issues such as race and gender in sufficient depth.

Others, whilst recognizing this, still value the experience of core sessions:

I've often gone home at the end of the day with a brain bubbling with a range of insights (sometimes frustratingly fleeting) which I desperately try to hold together.

Clearly, many secondees feel that they experience an increase in self-worth during the secondment and the core programme contributes towards this.

— I never felt that people really listened to me before. I used to stay quiet in school meetings. I didn't have the confidence to speak out.

— It's really increased my self-confidence. I used to be very nervous about standing up and talking to the whole staff at school but I find I am much better at it now.

— I'm much more positive in what I'm doing now. In my work, I feel much more confident in the educational processes I want to develop and I can be much more assertive in my actions and aspirations – very much more powerful.

We recognize that we can often provide the challenges and stimulus that generates this bubbling of ideas and that the secondment experience has been a powerful one for many secondees. The job of promoting and encouraging the critical reflection, engendered in the core programme, into school life resides not in any out-of-school INSET but in school themselves. In Chapter 4 of this volume other members of the tutorial team outline how this task is approached.

References

CLOUGH, P. (1989) *The Integration Rack: How Far Can You Go?* University of Sheffield, Division of Education mimeograph.

DEPARTMENT OF EDUCATION AND SCIENCE (1978) *Special Education Needs*, (The Warnock Report), London, HMSO.

DEPARTMENT OF EDUCATION AND SCIENCE (1984) *Records of Achievement: A Statement of Policy*, London, HMSO.

GREENFIELD, T.B. (1988) 'The Decline and Fall of Science in Educational Administration', in WESTOBY, A. (Ed.) *Culture and Power in Educational Organisations*, Oxford, OUP.

LAWRENCE, W.G. (1979) 'A Concept for Today : The Management of Oneself in Role', in *Exploring Individual and Organisational Boundaries* pp. 235–249, London, Wiley.

MORTON, D. and EVANS, J. (1987) *Management Development: A Study of the Needs of Headteachers*, Sheffield, LEA.

Douglas Finlayson et al.

SHEFFIELD LEA (1987) *Policy Statement on Record of Achievement and Experience*, Sheffield LEA, mimeograph.
WEDELL, K. (1985) 'Future Directions for Research on Children's Special Educational Needs', British Journal of Special Education, 12, 1, pp. 22–26.

Part Two
Practice and Progress

4
Supporting Change : The Role of the Tutor

Ian Anniss and Bob Gibbs

In September 1987, a team of ten tutors assembled to plan and implement on the essential principles of SCI. That team was drawn from a wide variety of backgrounds and experiences – there were two university lecturers, three polytechnic lecturers, an education psychologist, an adviser and three advisory teachers from the LEA and the GRIST evaluator for the LEA.

The accumulated experience of the team was considerable. There were many years' teaching experience ranging from pre-school to adult education, there were experiences of research and evaluation working with LEA, university and polytechnic education departments, working in industry and commerce and working for other agencies, for example, the MSC (now the Training Agency), NFER, Equal Opportunities Commission, Psychological Service, SCDC and SCIP. Most importantly however, the team members all had extensive experience of working with teachers and other adults on INSET programmes in a generic role, that is with the process of innovation, change and curriculum development, and not merely with a subject-specific input.

This team represented a multi-disciplinary and multi-dimensional approach to the task of supporting SFD secondees – this diversity and mixture of talents was the strength and the backbone of the tutorial team support. The other shared perspective within the team was one that offered a sharp critique of some of the INSET provision they had either been responsible for or participated in, and a growing dissatisfaction with traditional forms of INSET. The feeling was that there was a very limited and controlled impact upon schools as a whole and between schools.

This team of tutors brought a dynamic quality not only to the out-of-school programme but also to operating in the largely unoccupied middle ground between in-service and institutions, as well as working with secondees and their colleagues back at school. The quality of relationships as a prerequisite to effective learning was the central concern that ran through these actions.

To unravel the role of the tutor we propose –

* To give a brief introduction, setting the tutor role in the context of the present educational scene
* To outline some of the guidelines which have underpinned and informed the tutors' actions.
* To highlight elements of the tutoring role in practice.

The Tutor Role in Context

The present education system is in a state of flux. It is characterized by a confusion of purposes and priorities. There is unprecedented upheaval and change as teachers and administrators struggle to come to terms with major reforms and the demands that are being made on the system at all levels. Sometimes it appears that '... all that has been created is chaos, a muddle of organisational forms with no cohesion, no joint purpose and no relationship with each other, and no relevance to real educational needs.' (Havelock, 1983)

Out of this apparently infertile ground have emerged the urgent demands for the professional renewal and re-energizing of teachers with a growing awareness that staff and curriculum development required greater coherence and more detailed planning. In the past the challenge of planned change in schools has been met through staff turnover and the judicious appointment of an individual change agent. In the recent past, however, staff turnover has been minimal and schools have had to face the challenge of radical change within the human resources currently at their disposal. They must sort it out for themselves.

In Sheffield, SFS/SFD was brought into being to help teachers and schools to develop and respond to change. If SFD was to have a real and lasting impact on teachers, schools and children, it had to generate imaginative and effective methods of support to realize the human potential which was under-used in schools. This support was to be defined and acted upon by members of the tutorial team who had a brief to work with individual secondees, schools and clusters of schools.

The Baker reforms have been about effecting change through legislation and exercising power over particular groups. They have been characterized by a lack of consultation, by vilification campaigns against teachers, by the superimposition of tired industrial management models on the education service, and a celebration of the cult of the individual. Conversely, the reforms being advocated through the Sheffield Curriculum Initiative have been concerned with developing a process of consultation, collaboration and open communication to help teachers deliver a quality experience through the curriculum. The reforms called for the recognition and valuing of teachers' professionalism, the promotion of new paradigms of managing learning and a commitment to equality of opportunity. This, in turn, demanded a very different kind of support being offered to teachers and the development of positive relationships with schools.

Perhaps the most radical event within SFD has been the reconceptualization of INSET provision. The roots of this pre-dated SFD, having its origins in a variety of sources ranging from TRIST to the publication of documents like the one in Oxfordshire on *Effective Schools* (Oxfordshire LEA, 1988). INSET as it had been known in the 1970s was simply not good enough for the rapid changes of pace as experienced in the late 1980s. The *ad hoc* and fragmented INSET provision which targeted the lone teacher as the agent of change ('der einzelkampfer' see Chapter 7) was hardly a coherent recipe for development. Characteristically, the teacher nominated herself/himself for a particular course, usually experienced the course away from their place of work and returned to their host institution as the bright fish in the murky pond, who might spread a little light into the deeper recesses of the institution.

The reasons for a teacher or teachers attending a particular course were often far from clear, either from their perspective or from the perspective of the headteacher. There had usually been little negotiation or contracting around how individuals, groups or the school as a whole may benefit, there was often no clarity of how the experience might be integrated into the wider needs of the school, there was often scant regard paid to the difficulties of sustaining the innovation and implementation phases, and there was little evidence of on-going formative evaluation which informed practice.

In recent years, and partly as a response to the perceived limitations of traditional INSET, school-based INSET (SBI) has come to the fore. It is based on a notion that given some time and limited resources teachers can get their act together, in spite of an overload of change, reform and

legislation. There is a recognition that teachers' knowledge and expertise in a collective sense can be a powerful force for change, but it is
limited by the culture of the school and can be introspective in its
nature. There may be no challenge or limited alternative perspectives
offered or tolerated. Where the connections, relationships and tensions
implicit in a holistic view of INSET are uncovered and begin to be
understood a qualitively different kind of change occurs. There is a
discontinuity between what was and what is – issues around the themes
of values, power, structures, decision-making, ownership, responsibility and feelings become crucial to explore.

The role of the tutor as enacted in the context of SFD is a new
synthesis of functions and approaches. The SFD tutor aims to address
the criticisms of both traditional INSET and school-based INSET,
whilst drawing upon the strengths that are recognized in both. Certainly the role as it has been performed does not fit neatly into any
particular traditional role, such as adviser, advisory teacher or HE tutor.
The background experience of the tutorial team meant that there were
elements of these traditional roles present but that these have been set in
a new conceptual framework and understanding of the tutor role. The
notion of the insider/outsider consultant embraces best the spirit of the
tutor role and this view has had profound implications for the
day-to-day inter-actions and events which are part of the overall
programme.

Guidelines for Action

It will be useful to identify essential guidelines that inform the actions of
the tutor and differentiate it from others in the education service. We
consider there to be five broad guidelines underpinning action that are
based upon the principles outlined in Chapter Two. These are to do
with perspectives on learning; formative evaluation; demystifying the
curriculum; democratizing the process; improving communication and
contexts and cultures. What follows is an elaboration of these guidelines
and reference to the implications for the tutor.

Perspectives on Learning

As tutors we try to start from the point of valuing and engaging with
people's past and present experience. The learner becomes the central
focus of attention and the tutor cannot limit her or his task to the

transmission of her or his own understanding but must take the skills, knowledge and values of the learner as the point of departure. Developing this process of critical self-reflection is difficult and can be threatening. It is necessary to support people through this process and encourage the development of critical open relationships between participants, whilst developing the practice of learning as a co-operative process.

These critical open relationships might best be imagined as an infinite number of points upon a continuum covering the broad notion of support. At one extreme of the continuum is support which offers security and confidence so that people can make sense of, express and explore their own perspectives, opinions and feeling. At the other extreme of the continuum is support which offers a challenge and questions so that people can re-think, reshape and modify their views and behaviours. For the tutor this means relating closely to her or his secondees, on occasions literally spending days working through a particular piece of development.

This recognizes that learning is an inter-active process and that in an organizational context there will be different constructs of meaning and multiple realities. Helping teachers to develop the analytical tools to understand, to argue, to rethink and redefine their realities is to critically empower them to effect the changes in a relevant, intelligent and meaningful way.

For the tutor, further emphasis is placed upon the interdependency of the affective and the cognitive domains in learning. It is widely recognized that feelings play an essential part in the learning process, and yet possibly because of deeply embedded cultural beliefs and learned behaviour, many teachers operate more often than not using an empirical-rational model of learning. To go beyond the boundaries of the teachers' theory in action is to step into the unknown for both teacher and learner. For many teachers this is a nerve-racking experience, touching not only professional sensitivities, but often confronting the very soul of the teacher as a person and generating all manner of feelings ranging from fear to elation. Quite simply, it is important to realize that learning is as much about feelings as it is about intellectual potential or prowess.

Formative Evaluation

The belief that formative evaluation is an integral requirement for supporting change is another essential guideline. From the tutor perspective, evaluation is not the final task, remote, judgmental and too late to influence action. Rather, it is an on-going process which is open, accessible, part insider – part outsider and which informs or reforms action. The developments in evaluative approaches which can become a part of teachers' practice are an important source of evidence for supporting change. The development of the reflective practitioner is a move towards the development of the reflective organization, that is one that learns about learning.

> The professional responsibility of the teacher is to offer an approach to the task of ... [creating]..critical communities: to create conditions under which the critical community can be galvanized into action in support of educational values, to model the review and improvement process, and to organise it so that colleagues, students, parents and others can become actively involved in the development of education. The participatory democratic approach of collaborative action research gives form and substance to the idea of a self-reflective critical community committed to the development of education.
>
> (Carr and Kemmis, 1986)

Evaluation provides a means of connecting out of school experiences with in school experiences, of contrasting theory with practice, of reviewing transfer of learning from one situation to another, and of entering into dialectical relationships. Through evaluation is the opportunity to match and explore the relationship between the structural and human dimensions of the school – this can be disturbing! If perceived in this way, evaluation offers not only the means to illuminate successes and problems, but also the means to identify factors affecting those particular conditions. Evaluation can cast chronic problems in a new light, it can help to reframe a problem and in so doing offer new possibilities for intervention.

Demystifying the Curriculum: Democratizing the Process

We are guided by the belief that it is important to value teachers' knowledge, expertise and experiences in the context of curriculum change. Until recently the secret garden of the curriculum tended to be the prerogative of experts – HMI, advisers, higher education lecturers and researchers. It is only recently that teachers, particularly from the secondary sector, have gained some access and developed some wider understanding of curriculum issues and priorities. In one sense, the curriculum is now becoming public property under the various dimensions of ERA. Paradoxically, however, even given the illusion of curriculum control the broad direction of what is taught has been laid down by the national curriculum and how it is taught may well be determined by testing. The amount of real control and influence that can be exerted by parents and governors in defining the curriculum, as well as all the other rights and responsibilities they have been empowered to exercise under ERA may be very limited.

An essential part of the tutor's role is to demystify issues around curriculum development and change, and to break into teachers' taken-for-granted assumptions about not only the curricular content, but also the curricular processes which provide a worthwhile educational experience for young people. Our experience is that teachers often feel disconnected and disenfranchised from the processes of curriculum reform, they feel tied in curriculum knots -

> There is something I don't know
> that I am supposed to know.
> I don't know what it is I don't know,
> and yet am supposed to know,
> And I feel I look stupid
> if I seem both not to know it
> and not know what it is I don't know.
> (Laing, 1970)

The process of demystifying the curriculum requires the tutor to draw out of secondees their own interpretations and experiences of curriculum and to match this against the needs and entitlement of young people, the evidence and research of good practice, the frameworks of national curriculum, and the wider curriculum aims and objectives of the school and cluster. This is a complex process and has the inherent danger of remystifying the curriculum in an unhelpful way. If teachers and others are to engage in the processes of curriculum review and mapping, they must be offered the support and skills to participate actively and understand the implications beyond the limited representation of the curriculum which the review or map offers.

Inextricably linked with this curricular dimension is the need to encourage teachers to define collaboratively, agree and maintain some common values appropriate to their institution which form the basis for working together in achieving short-term goals whilst retaining a longer-term perspective. These common values might embrace such notions as open communication, shared decision making, respect for persons, power distribution and equality of opportunity.

> ...all those involved in educational change must be concerned with the manner as well as the matter of change. Many programmes of school-centred INSET are based on a myth : that one can simply sit down with others, work out policies, aims, strategies, etc and implement them according to rational procedures based on apparently rational agreements. Yet these take no account of the personalities of those involved, nor the effects on them of their involvement in the process of change. There may, for example, be conflicts over values, power and practicalities.
>
> (Patrick Easen, 1985)

Improving Communication

Crucial to the development of teachers in engaging with the processes of curriculum and staff development is communication in a variety of ways and contexts. As tutors we try to improve the quality and understanding of communication. Genuine communication is open and honest, and is concerned with real understanding and the sharing of experiences and feelings.

In general the concept of communication in schools is one that is limited and undifferentiated. That is to say that there is little importance paid to forms of communication beyond our habitual routines. Teachers are aware and sensitive to the communication that exists in a classroom, yet there appears to be less understanding of organizational communication in its many and varied forms. Communication in this sense is more than a simple exchange of ideas, it is the encouragement of a deeper exploration of issues and problems which helps to clarify what we are saying, and rather than creating dependency leads to independency of thought and action. The communication issue bites deeper in the context of SFD because of the many groups and forums were 'information' is exchanged, discussed and used to inform decisions.

> Information in organisations is often unreliable, biased, random, generated out of self-interest, and intentionally misleading. In short people in organisations lie.
>
> (Weick, 1983)

To go beyond this particular view of communication and to attempt to reduce the levels of distortion, the tutor engages with the secondee in a heuristic approach covering a range of areas where communication is a key variable, for example, classrooms, staff meetings, development groups, meetings with parents or industrialists and senior management meetings. For both tutor and secondee this means being sensitive to active listening, giving and receiving feedback, non-verbal communication and the processes of communication. The important principle in unravelling the complexities of communication is one that parallels the notion of 'INSET in context', that is that 'every datum becomes meaningful only when there is a relatum' (Boring, 1954). In other words, the relationship between organizational communication and organizational culture is an area that the tutor helps to explore.

Contexts and Cultures

The SFD programme gives teachers the necessary supported time out to reflect on their culture in context. The role of the tutor in this respect is to act as the critical co-investigator with the secondee, accessing information, encouraging analysis and re-examining commonly held assumptions. The aim is to stimulate response to the challenges implicit in the working contexts, which will not only raise the awareness of teachers, but also lead to the development of an informed theory-in-action and ultimately to an enhanced learning experience for pupils. For the teacher to bring about effective planned change in their schools, they need to become familiar with and come to understand the contexts and cultures within which they operate and which they might influence or change. This is applicable at two levels.

Firstly, there is a need to identify and lay bare the existing cultures and sub-cultures within their school to help understand why things are the way they are. This means becoming aware and sensitive to the legacies, myths and traditions of the school, and to begin to understand the norms, values and attitudes of themselves and their colleagues. Having partially explored the culture it is possible to take action towards creating a climate which nurtures advancement, growth and development, rather than one which discourages, inhibits and suffocates. This awareness is difficult to develop in teachers who live their lives in short, sharp bursts and remain totally immersed in their own culture.

Secondly, it is important to be exposed to and informed by the various political, social and economic pressures at local and national levels. In the age of ERA, schools are the pivotal point trying to fulfil national imperatives, whilst at the same time being responsive to local communities' aspirations. Indeed, successful interpretation of national priorities in the light of local needs can profoundly affect the quality and relevance of curriculum provision for pupils.

These then are some of the basic guidelines which inform the tutor as she/he works with and through a vertical cross-section of the school staff, LEA colleagues and representatives of the wider community. The style of support and the methods of investigation will vary according to needs and circumstances, but throughout the tutor will be attempting to 'get the best out of people' and 'helping people to help themselves'.

The Tutoring Role in Practice

This section will use the previously stated guidelines to elaborate on the role of the tutor, to give a brief overview of the various dimensions of the role, and to give something of a chronological exposition of a year in the life of a tutor, highlighting significant and critical events which we consider to characterize good practice. This is rather like trying to create order in a blurred world and it will be necessary for the reader to keep firmly in mind the guidelines which underpin the practice to help gain insights into the role of tutor.

As was stated earlier in this section, the role of the tutor is probably best described as the insider/outsider consultant. It would be wrong to think of this role as one dimensional. It is in fact multi-dimensional, a compendium of roles merged into one to respond to the demands of different situations. The tutor may be described as a consultant but encapsulated in that concept is a host of sub-roles – the tutor as teacher, as trainer, as catalyst, as expert, as counsellor, as facilitator, as manager, as learner, as confronter, as advocate, as defender, as organizer, as evaluator, as leader, as communicator, as politician, as diplomat, as confidant ... this does not mean that the tutor becomes all things to all persons. It does mean observing the guidelines as detailed previously and acting at times with courage and at other times with humility. In a metaphorical sense it means going beyond the chameleon game, accepting that at times the only intelligent course of action is to live with the norms of a particular situation but always retaining a duality of consciousness which means constantly exploring new avenues and possibilities and developing a fine sense of timing to make appropriate interventions.

These roles are not exclusive of each other and, for example, whilst it may be necessary to start a process off by playing the role of teacher, as part of the developmental process, the role changes to that of co-learner. This presents constant dilemmas for the tutor in terms of which role(s) do I adopt in which circumstances? How explicit do I make my role? When and how do I intervene? How do I make sense of the 'slice of reality' to which I have access? What is the most appropriate support role? In practice what happens is that the tutor tries to adopt the role(s) which seem to be the best course of action and in the best interests of all concerned at any given time.

It might help the reader to see the tutor role as a passage through various phases, each of which demands and requires different amounts of time, pace, input and intensity of effort. These phases can be seen as having four themes – Commissioning, Induction, Commission Development and Review, Preview and Evaluation. The attached model gives an indication of this cycle of events but is not definitive, indeed it may place limitations on conceptualising the reality of the role. The model should be perceived as a stepping stone towards fuller understanding of its complexities. The phases are not as distinct or clear as the model implies, and there may be, and often is, an overlap, an exploration beyond the particular phase or strong bonds and connections made between phases. This is particularly true of the Commissioning Phase, which has closely connected in-school/out-of-school subsets, and is often a time of creative turbulence for the secondee who may simultaneously still be coming to terms with particular aspects of the culture of the school from the induction phase, whilst starting the process of evaluation to further other parts of their work.

On the other hand there may be a fracture, a dislocation or a breakdown in the model and alternative strategies have to be considered – this may happen in the clarification of commissions in the induction period, when the reality of what is required only becomes apparent after some reflection. What the model does strongly indicate, however, is the strong interdependence between the constituent elements and the dynamic that exists between the tutor and the principal actors in the process. The model describes the human resource and the human technology available to support change.

School Focused Development Programme

CRITICAL PHASES FOR THE ROLE OF THE TUTOR .

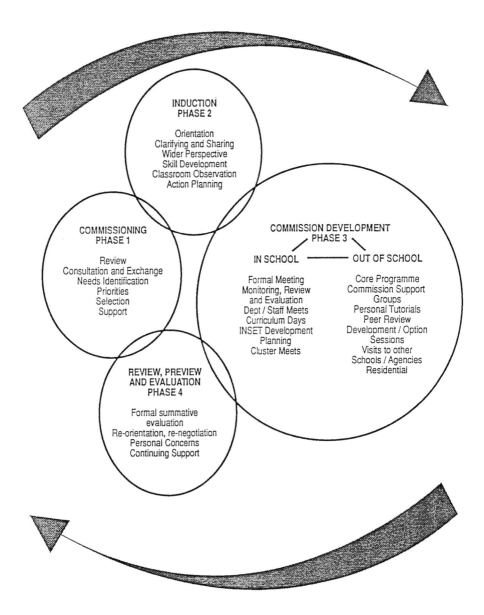

Commissioning Phase:

This is a planning stage where a wide range of school and LEA staff and the tutor meet in a variety of groups over a period of weeks to review recent developments at a school, cluster and LEA level, to identify particular needs and priorities at both a personal, curriculum and organizational level, to consider possible ways forward and to draw together some coherent plan of action which uses the SFD resource as part of the wider school staff and curriculum development plans.

The tutor acts as consultant to the different groups offering information, possible strategies, different forms of support, cross-fertilising ideas and clarifying how to get the best out of SFD. In this sense the tutor acts as the link and the flux between the past, the present and a variety of possible future scenarios. At the end of this process of review and consultation, a decision is made and the particular needs and priorities to be addressed are written up in the form of a loose contract. This is communicated to the LEA, who have overall responsibility for the initiative, and to the SFD team, who plan and co-ordinate the whole programme. In parallel with the commissioning process, decisions have to be made about which teachers to second, for how long and a definition of some broad parameters within which further refinement of their commission and other related work can take place.

Induction Phase

Ideally, by the end of the summer term prior to secondment, the main actors in the process and planning stage have a common understanding of the nature of the commission work to be undertaken and some idea of other benefits which might accrue from the secondments either in a direct or indirect way. Usually, at around this time, the tutor attached to the school will meet with the prospective secondees and school co-ordinator to outline basic information and respond to particular concerns regarding the imminent secondment.

At this stage the teachers often begin to feel a high degree of emotional turmoil, with a mixture of feelings, ranging from excitement to trepidation about the future prospects and expectations – 'How am I going to go about my commission? How can I disengage from my current preoccupations and feelings of guilt? I am looking forward to this, yet I am scared about...what? All these people seem very clear and articulate, how do I seem to them? This does not sound like a secondment as I understood it in the past? So that's what SFD is about! Can I survive?'

From this briefing emerges some better understanding of the philosophical underpinnings of SFD, greater clarity for secondees about the human and physical resources that are available to support them in fulfilling their commissions, and the agreement to a contract laying down some ground rules for future working – no 'put downs', authentic reflection, honest and open communication, confidentiality – and a commitment between the tutor, the co-ordinator and the secondees to honour the programme requirements and demands. This pre-programme briefing provides an opportunity for the tutor to listen and collect views about the kinds of issues to be addressed through and beyond the programme. Between the in-school briefings and the beginning of the year, the tutorial team operate in a flurry of programme planning, development of support networks, and updating on current initiatives and developments, for example, TVEI-E, Partnerships, ERA.

The first three weeks of the year are spent participating in an induction programme which the tutors plan, organize and deliver – the tutor acts as the facilitator to a variety of groups dealing with a range of issues. It is a time for the secondees to orientate themselves, to clarify, share and possibly re-define commissions, to take on a wider perspective, to develop new relationships, to practise and develop skills, to think about and discuss educational and personal issues. It is time to plan, to consider the implications of change and to visit other schools and take part in observing pupil learning. It is a three weeks rich in variety and experiences where tutors and secondees begin to develop a better understanding of each other, where hopes and fears are expressed and where the deep-seated values and beliefs we carry as teachers are challenged and reflected upon. It is the beginning of a process of transformation for both tutor and secondee which is the basis of work in the future. It is felt by many to be the dawn of an exciting period in their lives.

The euphoria of being out of school wears off. The induction weeks have finished – where now? The tutor and the secondees move on to analyze the situation they find themselves in. It is a period of exploration and critical co-venturing. Thinking and talking about such questions as:

— What do I already know that will help me develop my commission?

— What do I need to find out? Where can I find out? Who can help me? How can I best make use of the resources around me?
— How might I start the process of delivering my commission? What factors are going to influence the outcome of my commission? What might be the potential problems?

These questions and more form the basis for continuing conversations, debate and investigation between tutor and secondee and form part of the transition from induction to the development of the SFD experience.

Commission Development Phase

This is the most difficult period to describe as there are two subsets, in-school and out-of-school running simultaneously. At first glance it may seem no more than a period when there is time in school and out of school for secondees to pursue their own tasks, with some outside support and superimposed upon that, almost as a distraction, a course which bears no relationship with the day to day realities of schools. This would be a gross misunderstanding of this phase as the in-school and out-of-school activities have a dialectical relationship to each other, they are inextricably intertwined and interdependent.

To describe the significant characteristics and different arenas within which the tutor operates in the context of this phase, it is necessary to artificially separate the in-school and the out-of-school activities, although it must be stressed that in reality relationships are made between the two and they often spark off each other.

The essential elements which make up the out-of-school programme have been described earlier, and from the tutor's perspective these elements have particular significance and meanings. In many of these areas enormous help and guidance was offered by a wide network of advisers, advisory teachers, CAR tutors, Health Education Council staff, Sheffield Education Business Partnership (SEBP) staff, Sheffield Unified Multicultural Education Service (SUMES) staff, and other support teachers and agencies both within and beyond the LEA. The aims of the programme were:

- The provision of a core experience, which was in broad terms concerned with rethinking experiences and focusing on learning by addressing related issues and contexts, was planned, implemented and evaluated by the tutor team, with a sensitivity to the on-going needs of secondees.

- The breathing into life of commission support groups (CSGs) was also initially the responsibility of the tutor team. These CSGs were learning sets composed of teachers with common or similar commissions, for example, groups concerned with Community Education, Balanced Science, Guidance, and Learning and Assessment. The tutors or others assigned to different groups adopted a facilitatory and enabling role in the first instance, but over a period of weeks responsibility for the organization and running of the groups was passed over to group members.

- The tutor provides input and manages groups who have specific needs and these groups fall into two broad categories – cluster groups or option/development groups. The cluster groups tend to deal with the overarching concerns and developments within clusters of primary or secondary schools as they affect the majority of teachers. The group acts as a sounding board and as a clearing house at different levels in the school structures. The agenda is based on the particular issues of the moment and at times is prescribed to deal with specific areas of development. These other groups are much more specific in their purposes. Secondees identify particular needs they have or offers of useful inputs are made by the tutor team or associated colleagues. These groups concern themselves with issues such as classroom strategies, special needs, counselling, timetabling, health education etc.

- The final element of the programme involves the formal tutorial sessions. They may be held on a one-to-one basis or on a peer group basis. This tutorial time gives an opportunity to have a more intense and pertinent discourse between tutor and secondee about the experience as a whole and to challenge and support developments. The tutorial is intended to help sharpen up the progress on commissions and other work in a spirit of collaborative enterprise. For secondees who opt into a course of academic study towards a diploma or master's degree, the outcomes of the tutorial provide a positive contribution to their studies.

In a similar way the in-school dimensions of the tutor role have particular and special significance. The school is the crucible of change towards which are directed all the efforts and energies to support the process of growth, development and constant renewal at both the personal and organizational levels. The key to this part of the tutor role is communication and time. The tutor aspires to go beyond merely learning about the school by developing a level of intimacy which attempts to lead to a situation where she/he can be accepted as less threatening and thereby reduce any resentment or resistance. The tutor may work in different arenas. For example :

- Regular, fortnightly, review and dialogue meetings with secondees and school co-ordinators, setting the experiences, insights and expertise gained into context, monitoring progress and offering mutual help and support. Occasionally these meetings expand to involve headteachers, advisers and other colleagues and, in those circumstances there is a wealth of experiences and perspectives which provides a cornerstone for development.
- Beyond the review and dialogue meetings are other numerous possibilities and here the tutor has to be both selective and opportunistic. Gaining access to departmental or faculty meetings provides a valuable insight into the worlds beyond SFD and the tutor becomes very much a member of the meeting, listening, clarifying and, if requested, giving feedback.
- Secondees, as part of their commission related work, often ask for help in both the planning and implementation of workshops, meetings or INSET sessions. Why is this help needed? The secondees find themselves cast in the role of prophets in their own lands; this is often an unusual and unexpected role to play and one that requires great skill and sensitivity. The tutor adopts the role of critical friend giving help, where appropriate, giving confidence, even inspiration.
- This last 'arena' often provides a springboard into wider staff and curriculum development spheres of action. The tutor encourages the school to use her/him as a resource and thus may find herself/himself involved in curriculum days, full staff meetings and specific development groups, adopting a variety of roles ranging from expert to participant.
- In a more formal sense, the tutor becomes involved in a range of groups involved with cluster development. This will include the cluster management group, a forum including representation from headteachers, advisers, officers, careers

service, CAR and SFD, and may include a variety of other groups – for example, TVEI-E, Assessment and Guidance.

-   Finally, but not definitively, the tutor has some responsibility for helping the school become more self-reflective by modelling an approach which is participatory, collaborative and democratic. This means the tutor acting as both soother and irritant simultaneously, by problematizing the relationships between individual and organization, and theory and practice. It is adopting an 'emancipatory facilitation role' which provides,

the critical impulse ... towards the transformation of educational institutions ... not only in individual critical thinking but in the common critical enterprise of changing selves in order to change the institutions those selves generate through their joint practices of communication, decision making, work and social action.

(Carr and Kemmis, 1986)

The Review, Preview and Evaluation Phase

Throughout the period of secondment there has been a process of review and evaluation of a formative nature and as the cycle of development draws towards its crescendo there again emerges a host of pressures, priorities and demands. This represents a period of several weeks prior to the re-entry of secondees into school on a full-time basis and is an opportunity, in a formal sense, to look back and to consider various routes towards the future. It is also a time of valuing the experiences and making explicit the connections and tensions between those experiences.

The tutor aims to provide a structured framework to address the issues and concerns surrounding the personal and professional events over the last months and to map out where and how that human resource might be integrated into the heart of the school. The secondees address a range of questions – What I have learnt? How do I use this new learning? What have I valued this year? What has been successful/failed? Why? How do I feel now? What problems/concerns do I have about the future? How do I engage with colleagues on these issues? How are developments to be managed at the micro and macro levels? Where do I go from here? The responses to these and similar questions provide a rich and colourful tapestry of human endeavour and feelings –

an agenda is provided for the tutor and secondees to pursue with each other and, where appropriate, with a wider audience.

Part of this phase often highlights the problem of re-entry for secondees. This is a complex issue and has various facets which confuse the process of returning to school. In one sense, the secondees have never left school, therefore re-entry should not be such a problem. They have spent approximately half their time on secondment in school and maintained close relationships with colleagues and the day-to-day running of the school. From a tutor perspective, the problem is deeper and has a range of cross currents causing a degree of disturbance. There is a discrepancy in the pace and nature of the lived experiences of the secondees and the realities of development back in the school. There are 'frozen' images and perceptions between all parties, there is sometimes a reluctance on the part of the school to acknowledge the potential offered by the secondees. The tutor tries to navigate through these turbulent waters and offer a range of opportunities for people to recognize the concerns and to make best use of the human resource available. Suggestions are made to ease a passage through this phase, including discussion around areas such as reorientation, possible new roles, linking with other staff and curriculum development, in-school support and structured development time.

It will be clear that the implications and outcomes at this stage lead naturally into and feed the commissioning phase. It is never neat and tidy, but there are connections to be made and experiences to be built on. The tutor helps in weaving the connecting thread between the different parts of the staff, curriculum and organizational developments.

This is a glimpse of the action that characterizes the differing contexts within which the role of the tutor is played out. It is important to emphasize that these phases are not the entire sum of tutor activity, nor are they discrete pieces of action, nor are they based on a simple concept of change. These cameos of support represent some of the best models of tutor activity and practice – we do not always live up to our own expectations. Ultimately, there is one central purpose – to support in a relevant and meaningful way the provision of a quality comprehensive education for all.

Some Implications for the Future

This section will reflect on some implications and raise some issues and challenges for the role of the tutor and similar support roles both within the context of SCI and beyond.

As we move into a post-ERA period, the longer term effects of LFM, restructuring of LEAs and the shift in the balance of power to headteachers and governing bodies are still to be measured. LEAs find themselves in the bizarre situation of planning and orchestrating their own demise. For much of the time it seems that we are all working to someone else's agenda. Can we retain the principles and guidelines which we believe underpin the quality of INSET and educational provision? If we are seriously committed to the ideal of transforming pupils' experiences when all the pressure is on for the provision of conforming experiences – National Curriculum, testing etc. – how do we go about supporting teachers in this difficult task?

Within the context of SCI the future is difficult to predict, but there are some certainties. In the last three years, approximately 400 primary, secondary and tertiary teachers have been through the SFS/SFD experience, many more have had strong associations and contacts. The growing autonomy of schools under LFM may mean a drastic reduction in longer periods of time on secondment, but the powerful lessons from the SFD experience are ignored at our peril. We would support the view that change of any consequence will only happen when teachers are given time, structure, quality support, intellectual challenge and are trusted to manage the processes of change. Also, given that there will be an even greater premium on teacher's time, we see emerging new roles and relationships based upon some of the practice defined in this chapter. We envisage that the tutor role will become more generic, being located in two clear areas. Firstly, this will mean operating much closer to the action with schools and clusters of schools, fulfilling an in-house professional development consultant role, contributing to particular areas of development whilst retaining a sense of the whole school and cluster development plans. Secondly, continued active involvement and substantial contribution to other LEA initiatives beyond SFD – Partnerships, MST, Primary RAE, TVEI-E development, Inter-LEA evaluation, Appraisal, etc. – needs to be sustained and developed. This networking process has made the connections where none existed before and tested new structures to deal with the demands of sustaining and improving the educational provisions in Sheffield.

Beyond SCI, as will be seen by the final section of this book, Sheffield has attracted some keen interest in its professional development work. Requests for information have come from around the country and various parts of the world – some of this interest has come from the world of industry, business and commerce. What is the interest? Certainly the size of the operation takes some absorbing, but what has also attracted attention is the particular role played by tutors and the philosophy implicit in that role. It seems that many people in LEAs, schools and other organizations are searching for sense of vision and innovative practice which might help to improve not only the quality of educational provision, but also the quality of life for all engaged in that process.

We have learnt a great deal from friends and colleagues inside and outside Sheffield. We believe that sharing our experiences may go some way towards illuminating the various support roles being enacted by officers, advisers, advisory teachers, curriculum consultants, head-teachers and teachers in schools. In this context, we hope that the role of the tutor as played out in SFD contributes something to inform and inspire some re-thinking of the support roles in education.

In the light of the recent massive changes in education, we believe that the positive support of teachers in the coming decade will be *the imperative*. We are concerned that there is already a strong view at a variety of levels in education, that teachers will be expected to handle, with minimal support, the demands of the National Curriculum, testing, a host of cross-curricular themes, TVEI-E, constant reorganiz-ation and, the not insubstantial task, of managing the learning of classes of demanding young people. Unless the professional entitlement of teachers is given the highest priority and they are offered support of quality, then we fear that teachers will, quite sensibly, discharge their duties in a de-personalized, functional and uncritical way. The experi-ence for all will be impoverished.

Given these observations and the quest for different positive and open relationships between schools and the LEA, perhaps the biggest challenge is whether all interested parties can keep their heads and retain the sense of a common purpose and continue to provide development opportunities for teachers, rather than going for quick, cheap short-term solutions which are forced on headteachers from a pragmatism born of reality. One further issue this raises is 'who supports the supporters?' Certainly our experience is that if schools are to be extended the kind of support exemplified in SFD, then attention has to be paid to the personal and professional development of the supporters with more emphasis on working in teams, developing consultancy skills and processes, understanding development and change, taking risks and learning from mistakes, sharing power and taking responsibility, and, crucially, retaining a shared vision of how education might become an enlightening experience.

Finally, it seems to us that we are faced with some simple choices that have profound and long term implications. If, on the one hand, we become like straws in the wind, the totally responsive trainers, lost in the culture of silence, the free traders of the education world where the market forces dominate, cultural contortionists trying to respond to every conflicting demand placed upon us, then we have fears for the future. On the other hand, we can take up a position that supports the principles and guidelines expounded in this book, a position that helps people to know themselves, to know others, to understand a little more the complexities of living now and the possibilities for the future. If we become people who take action that humanizes, who act locally and think globally, who demonstrate a little more courage in the face of adversity, then we may just have a chance of contributing through education towards the caring and confident communities of tomorrow in which we hope our own children will flourish and grow.

References

ARGYRIS, C. and SCHON, D. (1978) *Organisational Learning : A Theory of Action Perspective*, London, Addison Wesley Publishing Company.

BENNIS, W., BENNE, K. and CHIN, R. (1985), *The Planning of Change*, New York, Holt Rinehart Winston.

BORING, E.G. (1954) 'The Nature and History of Experimental Control', *American Journal of Psychology*, No. 67.

BLAKE, R. and MOUTON, J. (1976) *Consultation*, London, Addison Wesley Publishing Company.

CARR, W. and KEMMIS, S. (1986), *Becoming Critical*, Lewes, Falmer Press.

CONOLEY, J.C. (Ed.) (1981) *Consultation in Schools – Theory, Research, Procedures*, New York, Academic Press.

EASEN, P. (1985) *Making School-Centred INSET Work*, Beckenham, Open University/Croom Helm.

HANDAL, G. and LAUVAS, P. (1987) *Promoting Reflective Teaching – Supervision in Action*, Milton Keynes, Open University Press.

HAVELOCK, R.G. (1983) 'The Utilisation of Educational Research and Development', in Horton and Raggatt, *Challenge and Change in the Curriculum* Sevenoaks, Open University Press.

HOPKINS, D. and WIDEEN, M. (Eds), (1984) *Alternative Perspectives on School Improvement*, Lewes, Falmer Press.

LAING, R.D. (1970) The Poem 'Knots', London, Tavistock Publications.

OXFORDSHIRE COUNTY COUNCIL (1988), *Effective Schools 1988 – A report by the Chief Education Officer*, Unpublished LEA document.

WEICK, K.A. (1983) 'Organisational Communication – Towards a Research Agenda', in Putnam and Pacanowsky, *Communications in Organisations*, Beverly Hills, Sage Publications.

5
Given Time: Developing Practice

Pat McAteer and Linda Power with Kath Aspinwall

Setting the Scene

In this chapter two teachers who were seconded to the SFD programme in 1987/88 describe their experiences. These two complementary accounts delineate the work that they and the staff at their schools carried out in the fulfilment of their commissions and give an insight into the ways in which they experienced their time as secondees.

The commissions, which focused on the investigation and instigation of appropriate adult and community education in a secondary school and the development of oracy skills in primary children, are just two of the many tasks that have been carried out as part of SCI. However, they share some common and more general characteristics with other activities in other schools which will be drawn out at the beginning and end of their accounts.

The school-focused nature of the tasks and the fact that the LEA suggested the direction, but in no way the substance of any development makes the secondees themselves particularly crucial. As is stressed in other chapters, the way in which secondees and their commissions are chosen by their colleagues and the consequent commitment to these decisions is always important. However, the secondees themselves, their approach to their work, their ongoing relationships with staff, their general credibility within a school are all important factors affecting what happens.

In order to develop an understanding of what secondment means to the teachers involved during their secondment year and after 're-entry', I, as the evaluator of the project, interviewed one first-wave secondee from each secondary school and one fifth of the primary secondees at the beginning and end of their year's secondment and in the Spring term after their return to full-time teaching. The findings of this study show that the experience is a significant intervention in the teachers' careers.

A more detailed account of the reactions of secondees can be found in evaluation documents cited in the Endpiece of this volume but these can be summarized as follows:-

- All secondees, in every interview, stressed the great value of time out of the classroom to reflect on and question their practice. This time for reflection had at all times to be counter-balanced against the pressure for action, the need to be seen to 'deliver' and the endemic busyness of teachers. Many secondees found this balance hard to maintain at times. Some later expressed regret at being too preoccupied with their task, sometimes feeling this may have been at the expense of developing a deeper and wider understanding of the issues involved.
- The teachers enjoyed the combination of challenge and support they experienced during secondment. This was found to be very stimulating if not always comfortable and enabled them to examine long held assumptions and to question their practice in ways that proved to be developmental.
- The opportunity to visit other schools and authorities and other classes within one's own school was highly valued and perceived to be beneficial to both visitors and visited. Some-times secondees covered for other staff so that they too could make visits. Observing different approaches functioning suc-cessfully elsewhere could prove a key intervention in the process of changing practice in a school.

Through such experiences secondees have found themselves to be developing personally and professionally in several ways. Most claim to have increased their understanding of themselves, how they relate to, and work with pupils, and other staff, and how their behaviour affects others' response to them. A considerable increase in professional understanding is also claimed, both in the area of particular commis-sions, and about educational issues in general, including the way in which schools as organizations make an impact upon those working within them. There is evidence of more understanding of, and therefore more sympathy for, other staffs' concerns and this often includes those of senior management. Almost all secondees felt more confident at the end of their year, some to a marked degree (one or two suggest they were quite confident enough already!). Most see themselves to have been regenerated by the experience and return to full-time teaching empowered, remotivated and with greater clarity about the principles and purposes that underpin their practice. These statements are not unsubstantiated, being frequently confirmed by tutors, heads, co-ordinators and advisers, one of whom spoke of witnessing an 'exponential growth'.

Some secondees can anticipate their return to full-time teaching with some apprehension but it is rare for anyone to experience more than short-term difficulties. Some teachers find they have raised their expectations of themselves to unrealistic heights and experience some disappointment and guilt when they cannot live up to their own expectations. The way the whole school responds to re-entry is also significant. If there is little recognition of the new skills that have been developed and little or no chance of the work being extended, or conversely, if secondees are allowed or encouraged to take on too many new responsibilities (often without promotion) there are obvious difficulties. However, in general schools are learning to balance the need to recognize and value new potential without endowing 'star status' on teachers who may already be seen by their colleagues to have been privileged.

At this point we will move away from general statements about secondment to the particular accounts of two secondees.

SFD – A Secondary Teacher's View: Pat McAteer

In the SFD secondment programme 1987–88 my commission was to investigate the area of adult and community education with the intention of introducing some appropriate activities within the school to create closer links with the community. As a modern languages teacher I had been working in the classroom situation for twelve years. Although I had attended courses every year they had, by and large, been short courses provided by the LEA; or longer courses taking place outside school hours. I looked forward to the year as an opportunity not only to stand back from the classroom teaching but also as a challenge represented by looking at an area of work in which I was interested, but which was also a new departure for me.

Pat McAteer and Linda Power with Kath Aspinwall

Early Days

In spite of an earlier preliminary meeting I remember feeling apprehensive on the first day. I had spoken to colleagues who had followed the SFS programme, and was starting out with certain expectations, but there was generally a feeling that things might be different as fewer teachers were involved, and the first year's experience might influence the design of the secondment. The feeling of going into something 'unknown' created both expectancy and anxiety.

It was evident from the beginning of the induction programme that a lot of thought had gone into the way in which the course would be operated, and a certain pattern was laid down early. There were very few whole-group sessions involving large numbers. Working in smaller groups and sub-groups enabled us to get to know each other and the tutorial team, ensured that everyone could contribute and feel comfortable in doing so. A residential experience in Filey with its participation in activities with colleagues in different circumstances and surroundings with the help of experienced facilitators bound the groups together.

Time was spent on commission-related work and the SFD programme work. All secondees followed the same core days within their tutor groups where issues such as the management of change, gender, the politics of education, race etc. were considered. The core days were not necessarily related to the commission, but provided an opportunity to learn more about certain questions, to discuss with colleagues and to raise the general level of awareness. Some I enjoyed immensely and gained from. Some made me feel uncomfortable or guilty about my own complacent attitude. A good guest speaker often made a great deal of difference to one's receptiveness to, or interest in, a new idea and I particularly recall a day entitled 'The Global Perspective' in which the entire group participated actively and with enjoyment, due to the enthusiasm of the guest. At times during the year, particularly when commission-related work was making urgent demands upon my time, I felt that the core day was obtrusive and a fringe activity. In retrospect, I regret this as I feel that it is useful to look at the general picture in the field of education as well as focusing on the particular.

Support

The commission support groups, made up of secondees with similar or related commissions, was productive in respect of school-based work. The ambience was friendly and supportive and an atmosphere of mutual trust was quickly established. Some of the most fruitful outcomes resulted from informal discussion within the 'Community' group. In fact we still meet once or twice per term in one another's schools to exchange news, ideas and information. A further source of help and advice came through the school tutor who was available for us throughout the year.

In terms of the commission, the early part of the work was concerned with developing my own concept of community education, finding out something of the underlying philosophy, looking at the forms it takes and at what is considered good practice within the field. Initial contacts and invitations made earlier in the year at the Community Education Conference were followed up and led to exploration of the working of adult education institutions, schools, colleges, community centres and other agencies involved in the delivery of community education.

Regular contact with the school co-ordinator and the head was made, by appointment, usually on alternative weeks. These sessions took the form of briefings, discussions, indications for development of work and how it might fit into the pattern of planning for the school as a whole. The individuals concerned were supportive and encouraging throughout the year, and from observing and talking to colleagues this was one of the decisive factors in the success of any commission.

A series of individual interviews with staff produced a generally positive view of community development with many staff willing to accept adult learners in classes, and keen to encourage adults as helpers. There was a feeling that parental involvement in secondary schools was desirable. Actually interviewing staff was something new for me. I found them open, frank and prepared to make time even when under great pressure of work. I learnt more about them as individuals and appreciated the opportunity to talk to those in the school with whom I had not been closely involved.

In school I became involved in a variety of activities related to the commission. I was asked to report at staff meetings, to make reports to a sub-committee of the governors, to organize with another secondee a meeting of our joint staffs and to address a meeting of the clergy from city parishes. I joined working parties which I considered might further the progress of the commission, e.g. access to one-year courses, and I became a member of the Joint Advisory Board whose membership was composed of staff from two schools in consortium at sixth-form level. An evaluation of the work of this board was carried out in the second term by myself and a seconded colleague.

Following work on provision for under-fives, an afternoon course for CPVE students was organized. I became a member of the steering committee to establish a Junior Club for disabled children aged 7 to 14, using our Sports Hall one evening per week, and involving the co-operation of several agencies (Sheffield Recreation, Community Transport, South Yorkshire and Humberside Sports Association, Sheffield Polytechnic). I also became involved in meetings with representatives from the Arts Council with a view to obtaining grants needed to extend the range of activities available to the Junior Club members.

When using the term community education one is not merely talking about formal adult education classes, but using it as an umbrella term to cover any kind of activity in which groups come together, interact and learn from each other. Identifying certain target groups e.g., women, the unemployed, the under-fives, the elderly, was a useful means of investigating provision and finding out how to get started. During the year, contact was made with many agencies in the statutory and voluntary sectors and included Help the Aged, a 16-60's Club run in a Doncaster school, lunch clubs, open learning centres, the Early Childhood Education centre, Parent-Toddler groups, crèches, Family and Community Services, MSC, Job Clubs, the Community Education Development Centres, community schools in Coventry, Liverpool and Bradford, various branches of the advisory service, FE colleges, parent workshops, etc. I attended courses and conferences pertinent to the study, e.g. Adult Basic Education, Towards Community Education, Network days, a study day on community education organized by the LEA. A picture began to emerge about the costs, staffing, organization, and implementation of the various activities and their potential for use in the school situation.

In the summer term a project to involve parents in the life of the school by inviting them to participate in a range of short courses was implemented. Staff worked on a voluntary basis and made offers of courses which were publicized. Parents were invited to bring a relative or friend and attended sessions ranging from word-processing to jewellery making. There was evidence to suggest that the experience was enjoyed by teachers and adults alike.

Personal and Professional Development

The personal and professional benefits of secondment became evident as the year progressed, the chief one, always mentioned by secondees, being time – time for investigation, for visits to schools, for talking to colleagues, for reading the literature available, for reflection and for planning. I found myself regaining many of the ideals which I had set out with as an optimistic young teacher, and becoming more positive in my attitudes. I remember also having a distinct feeling of guilt that I did not feel exhausted by the weekend in a way that had virtually become the norm for me as a teacher! The feeling of being stimulated by new ideas, people and places created new interests and renewed old ones. The ways of working on core days and in CSG and the necessity of working with groups in school helped me to develop more confidence, especially in communicating with others. The opportunity to look at something new has opened up new areas for professional development and has widened my horizons and the award of the diploma is also a professional advantage in career terms. There are drawbacks also to secondment – the feeling of being solely responsible, the uncertainty about what will happen, the obstacles encountered, the anxieties associated with new situations and roles and the demands they make. These can turn secondment into a stressful experience.

There was a good deal of discussion about fears related to re-entry to school. In practice, I find school life creates its own rhythms and once back in the midst of it there is not much time for thought. There are stresses associated with the expectations of others, the pressure to 'deliver' or 'produce' something and it is very easy to assume total responsibility for outcomes in school.

Looking Ahead

In my own school the practical outcomes have centred around looking at our current situation and considering the way ahead, bearing in mind what was possible without additional resources or finance to the mutual benefit of our students and our community. Staff willingness to accept adult learners alongside the pupils was a way forward, and there has been some uptake from parents, and further enquiries about classes oversubscribed by pupils. The experience of the adults, their fellow students and the teachers will be monitored and evaluated to help in future planning.

Looking at local needs and provision, the decision to develop in the area of under-fives arose from the proximity of a feeder primary school.

Contact was made with the Under-Fives Advisory Service, the Pre-School Playgroups Association, playgroup leaders from another local group and with the head of the primary. The community education group which had started in school in September formed a sub-committee to work on the project and generated many useful ideas. We envisaged a curriculum link in this group with the fifth year childcare students, and the psychology teachers also expressed interest from the child development point of view. Choosing a room, checking it out for safety, planning access to the building, advertizing through the primary school and locally, following up any possibility of gathering equipment and toys, and planning activities was a very time-consuming process. The group began in November and is now becoming established. The sight of the parents and their children now seems to be accepted as normal on Monday morning.

Recently, three CPVE students have become interested in the group and have asked if they could help within the group and with fund-raising. The children themselves now look forward to coming and the parents appreciate the opportunity for adult conversation and have been delighted with the interest shown by older pupils.

In the sixth form a community service option has been established with students participating in a range of activities including giving support to first years in the classroom at our school, visiting primary schools to help in drama, PE, paired reading schemes, art and craft activities and visiting an elderly person once a week. Although a new initiative, it has been popular with students who are keen to broaden their horizons and do something new and challenging outside the classroom.

Use of structures within the school, such as the PTA, can also enhance the community aspect of work. At a recent meeting, parents offered their services to the pupils for careers talks and interview experience, both of which will be invaluable to the pupils and will involve others in the life of the school. The Junior Club continues to run and will celebrate its first birthday in May. Students on community service have become involved and two pupils of the school participate as members of the club.

Future plans include the involvement of the elderly in the school, again looking at possibilities not requiring funds. Ways forward, especially those which would also open up opportunities to pupils, will be on the agenda of the community education group. The need to be more outward looking is also of concern and ways of 'reaching out' to our community will also be explored.

I am grateful for having had the chance to be seconded and feel convinced that all teachers, especially those with several years of classroom experience, would derive enormous benefits from a similar opportunity both on a personal and professional level thus enriching themselves, their pupils and their schools.

A Primary Teacher's View: Linda Power

In the Summer term 1987, our inner city middle school was offered the chance of a teacher secondment to the SFD programme. A staff working party was established to identify the school's priorities for curriculum development. Language development dominated the discussions. The staff expressed concern over the development of oral skills across the curriculum. Many of our children seemed to find it difficult to clarify a statement or to substantiate an answer to a question. The staff welcomed the chance of a secondment and it was recognized at the outset that it was to be the staff's commission with the secondee used as facilitator. The headteacher expressed the need for all the staff to be involved and this certainly proved to be important during the year to enable 'change' to take place.

During the Autumn term, I was able to visit other schools to observe their language schemes in operation, to familiarize myself with current research and to consult with other professionals. The information was fed back to, and discussed with, the staff in regular SFD staff meetings. These meetings were important as a means for the secondee to maintain contact with all the staff and to negotiate the direction of the commission. They were held after school using directed time. However, I felt it important to meet only when the need arose because the staff's time was valuable.

Each week I tried to speak informally to each member of staff. This helped to maintain relationships already established and provided an opportunity to discuss the commission. I established regular meetings with a colleague who had been nominated as my school co-ordinator. Her role was invaluable as it helped me to keep in touch with the general mood of things, and to plan and administer the activities related to the staff SFD discussions. The headteacher also played a supportive role in discussing the projects undertaken and any problems arising from them. From my work during the Autumn term I realized that in order to develop and increase oracy across our curriculum we had to:

1 Increase and reinforce experiential work.
2 Develop co-operative group work.
3 Establish and evaluate 'effective' teaching methods.
4 Examine pupil and teacher attitude to group work and oracy.

The work in school over the year centred around these four points and the commission became much more than curriculum development; staff development became a high priority. Many influences would affect the decisions we had to make and I realized that a slow non-threatening approach was needed to get any change in school at all. Some of the staff were very open to new ideas, others were less so.

Work in the Autumn Term

I worked with twelve staff and we made a collection of successful ideas we'd used in the classroom to promote 'talk'. Some of these ideas were developed during the term with teachers reporting their successes, or failures, if they wished to our meetings. Post-holders within the school also catalogued existing resources in their curriculum area that could be used to promote 'talk' and lists were circulated to all staff. We also tried out activities that I had observed in other schools and some of these became a regular feature of our school curriculum. Things began to 'snowball' with many staff bouncing ideas off me. Some gave me written accounts of their lessons or tapes of children talking. The SFD staff meetings became more relaxed as staff were prepared to talk about their experiences.

I met our first school staff, who expressed a desire for more contact between our pupils, so some M4 children went into their school to read storybooks with the younger children. Some of the children also worked on a list of ground rules for good 'group' discussion, and 'show and tell' activities, in which children show and talk about their work to different audiences. Contact increased not only between year groups, but between first and middle school classes.

A language questionnaire was answered by every middle school child to enable us to discover the pupils' views on 'language'. The results and ensuing discussion helped the staff to reflect somewhat on their own practices. I met the four year groups individually to discuss the term 'oracy', what it meant to them and their pupils, and what skills would be needed to develop it. From these discussions the staff agreed upon seven broad aims and acceded that pupils would have different starting points and make different rates of progress within these.

After thorough consultation with the staff, they completed a diary sheet for a week which revealed the methods, frequency and curriculum areas in which they promoted talk. The aim of this was to give me a baseline of present practices. However, after quantifying the data, it appeared that many staff had stretched phrases like 'pupil talk' and 'co-operative group work' to their limits in order to fill up their diaries. My perceptions of these terms obviously differed and therefore I felt that it was essential to establish a 'common language' before we went any further.

A joint INSET day with our first school was held to facilitate this. It focused on different approaches to cross-curricular co-operative group work, the role of the teacher in these; and it explored some of the learning processes we go through, emphasizing the importance of 'talk' within these. Written and oral comments from the INSET day led to further discussions where a common understanding of the term 'pupil talk' and 'co-operative' group work was reached. The staff had given very positive feedback and I felt that we were ready to move on.

Work in the Spring Term

In our first meeting we looked at the term 'effective teacher' from a holistic point of view. We hoped to develop a more collaborative approach to teaching and during the term the staff were encouraged to consider self-appraisal and to think about the question 'Are you carrying out the teaching strategies which you intend?'

Using the experience of the previous term and the INSET day, all the staff were released for two separate hour sessions to work with, and observe, a group of children while I taught the remainder of their class. They were to plan some co-operative group work that would promote pupil talk in two different subject areas. This variation was to ensure that they did not only try out 'safe' subjects but tried to boost their confidence in another curriculum area. I stressed that my role was one of temporary facilitator as I did not want the introduction of co-operative group work to be dependent on my presence. We decided to choose some work with an end product to make the sessions relevant to the pupil but stressed that it was more important to observe the group processes. At the end of both the sessions, the teachers filled in an assessment sheet. This was only semi-structured, outlining a few questions to think about during the observation exercise, e.g. Did all the children participate equally? Did you intervene a lot? Their comments proved reflective and focused. They questioned their teaching style and tried to evaluate the importance of the 'group selection' and 'pupil talk'.

The pupils involved also filled in an assessment sheet in which they graded their ability in group skills according to certain criteria laid down. They also had to answer the question 'Did you enjoy group work?' and 'why?' All the children graded themselves highly but they found 'waiting their turn' and 'using others' suggestions' the most difficult skills. The staff agreed with the children's comments and found the activity very productive and worthwhile. The main issues to emerge over the term were those of group composition, suitability of task and pupil assessment. These were considered again in the Summer term.

I chose the research techniques mentioned because I did not want the staff to feel that I was assessing them in any way. Having been at my present school for several years, I had established good relationships with the staff and I did not want to make the staff uncomfortable or uneasy about the changes we were implementing. I was also very aware that I would be returning to teach alongside them the following year and in order to further develop any initiative it was crucial to maintain goodwill. It was also important not to increase the staff's workload with time-consuming methods of research. Many staff began to develop their own group activities to promote oracy and some contributed to our SFD staff meetings. Not all the staff participated with equal enthusiasm, but everyone had been involved.

Work in the Summer Term

Nine out of twelve staff involved me in their work this term which ranged from experimenting with group work, recording oral work in a variety of ways, children planning activities and further observation. The staff timetabled me for hour-long sessions depending on their needs. However, the theme of 'group composition' ran through all their work. The staff completed an assessment sheet at the end of their sessions to identify how this variable affected their plans and the pupils' work. The pupils also filled in the same self-assessment sheet as before but with the added open-ended question 'How do you like the group to be made up?' Their findings led to much discussion and reviewing of practice in the classroom. By being involved in the research and the evaluation process, staff awareness was heightened. This was revealed by their actions, their comments and the headteacher's observations. Pupils also expressed a positive attitude towards co-operative group work.

Outcomes of the Year

Over the year the research highlighted many things: staff anxieties about change to established work patterns, the need for more exploration into 'how children learn', the pressures teachers work under (time, curriculum, organizational) and the awareness of the social skills needed to work in a group.

Things began to 'mushroom' in school throughout the year and have continued to do so. We have held a joint 'book week' and other joint INSET days with our first school. Liaison between the two staffs has increased with more informal discussion about curriculum issues taking place. More 'show and tell' activities have continued between year groups and schools. Oral activities are now planned on termly planning sheets and the staff are trying to increase provision for children to have different 'audiences' for their work. Many initiatives from last year have been continued by the staff, and I have five further LEA days with supply cover to work in school to develop these. A primary oracy group started last year has continued to meet. This involves local schools who meet to discuss ideas to promote oracy and to explore a variety of current issues on the subject.

Progress and change are gradual processes, often slow to develop, but I feel that through the SFD secondment our school made a good start on the process of increasing oracy across the curriculum and of reviewing and improving our existing practices.

Personal Reflections

The year provided me with the unique opportunity to meet and discuss educational matters with teachers ranging from nursery to secondary schools. I gained an overview of educational practices throughout the city and was able to visit numerous schools across the educational perspective. The organization of the SFD programme provided the secondees with a non-threatening but stimulating environment where we could discuss and evaluate current educational initiatives, re-assess our own teaching styles and thoughts, conduct research and air our own views. The audience was always supportive and criticism always constructive.

Many techniques used by the tutors to manage a group, to establish good relationships and to help us re-assess our own practices proved useful in SFD staff meetings at school. My confidence received a terrific boost which enabled me to run meetings and INSET days and to promote discussions. I had time to look more closely at my own objectives and I became more conscious of the staff's problems and began to realise what an inward looking place a school could be. It is so easy to narrow your horizons as you become absorbed with the day-to-day programme of school life.

The experience on the SFD programme certainly renewed my enthusiasm and inspired me. They made me more aware of problems existing in schools and gave me many ideas to help to motivate staff and initiate or further curriculum development.

Conclusion

Many of the points from the start of this chapter have been reflected in, and clarified by, the secondees' accounts but there are one or two more points to be made.

Both teachers refer to the help and support they have received from their heads and co-ordinators. Visible but sensitive support from senior management has proved to be a significant factor in the success or otherwise of any development. Staff tend to be less inclined to take seriously any task that they do not believe to have the support of senior management although support from the top is not enough in itself. The two accounts also demonstrate very clearly the contribution of other staff in school. Accepting that some staff will always respond with more enthusiasm than others, in most cases the amount of very real practical support and sharing of the task has been impressive, more than might have been expected at a time of general low morale in the teaching profession.

The insights offered by just two of the many secondees demonstrate the potential of school focused secondments. The benefits of the secondment are spread more widely than to the individual teacher. However, the personal and professional growth in the secondees themselves demonstrated in this chapter suggested that the sharing of benefit is not at the expense of the teacher concerned. The programme and the relationship with the school tutor offer to secondees the opportunity to work in a way that is both supportive and yet challenging, requiring them (should they not already be so inclined) to examine existing practice and pupil experience, to explain and justify their thinking and to be self questioning. As this challenge takes place within a supportive and collaborative climate, creative thinking is a real possibility.

6
Heads or Tails: The Ten-sided Coin

Bob Driskell, Graham Evans, Jenny Frankish, Keith Pollard and Charles Sisum

The first intimation to headteachers that Sheffield LEA was about to launch a major curriculum initiative came in Bill Walton's talk at a secondary heads' meeting and the subsequent circulation of his letter to schools in December 1985. The CEO's ideas were greeted with considerable enthusiasm and some excitement. Heads felt that the LEA was responding to the thinking and questioning that was going on in schools and offering to give considerable impetus to changes and developments that were already being considered or attempted. Since this time the pace of change has accelerated and we are aware that our role and the way that our schools are managed is one of the key factors in deciding how ideas about practice are generated, responded to, developed and carried through. Changes of the magnitude being experienced cannot be managed with a little tinkering to the system. Further impetus has recently been provided by the possibility of TVEI Extension and, to some extent, by the passing of the 1988 Education Reform Act, ERA, although we have considerable reservations and anxieties about some aspects of the latter. As has been indicated in earlier chapters, change to the school curriculum and the process of staff development necessitate organizational and structural changes which inevitably impact upon the role and person of the head. We also find ourselves changed by our experiences.

As the headteachers writing this chapter we represent each of the different initiatives that come under the umbrella of the Sheffield Curriculum Initiative, SCI – SFS/D, primary and secondary, CDI and TVEI. We also represent the staff and pupils of our schools, which are named at the end of the chapter, and from which the examples we offer are taken. In this chapter we intend to draw together a picture of what has been happening in schools as a result of SCI, in the context of the national developments, in particular the ERA. We will consider the effect of SCI on staff, its impact on the curriculum and pupils' experience of schooling, the involvement of parents and governors and the changes to the ways schools are organized and managed. Lastly, we will reflect on how we, as head teachers, have been and are being affected by what is happening, what the experience means for us.

The Effect on Staff

The proportion of staff who have been radically affected by SCI developments varies from school to school. As we have seen in Chapter 5, in all schools the experience has had considerable impact on the secondees themselves and schools have benefited as a result. Secondees have found renewed enthusiasm, increased energy and confidence and developed new skills. These have been invaluable in the context of the Curriculum Days and more generally within the schools.

The quality of secondees has proved to be a key factor in the successful development of commissions. Their relationship with other staff and their sensitivity of approach has proved crucial. We have all been impressed by the number of occasions that we have seen secondees handling difficult situations with tact and skill or generating interest and enthusiasm with groups or individual colleagues. The way each school handled the selection of secondees has had considerable impact on the way their colleagues have responded to them. Where staff have been involved in deciding the way in which secondees will be chosen, have been carefully and openly consulted about the nature of the commissions and where these commissions are part of a longer-term development plan, everyone has benefited from this process. Where this has not happened secondees have found themselves, initially at least, at a disadvantage. The importance of staff ownership of what is happening has, in some cases at least, been painfully learned. There are also 'critical times' for development and getting both the timing, and then the pace, right is very important and secondees bear some, but not all, of the responsibility for how this is handled.

Heads clearly have a supportive role to play. Even though a school may have an organizational framework and an approach to management which is deemed 'open' and consultative, in the eyes of many staff it will be the headteacher who is seen as the keeper of the school's 'norms', values, aspirations and direction. Secondees' morale and effectiveness are greatly enhanced if the headteacher is seen and heard to identify with the aims and objectives of the secondment task.

In-school co-ordinators have been identified in each school and have played a valuable role in supporting secondees and providing a consistent link between them and the other staff. In most schools there are very useful, regular weekly or fortnightly meetings between secondees, the co-ordinator and the school tutor (see Chapter 4). In almost all cases the co-ordinators are deputy or assistant heads, although other senior staff are included, particularly when it is thought to be helpful to involve a past secondee in the role. With the exception of the TVEI schools, where the co-ordinators have a full-time secondment to the post, the work has to be added to existing responsibilities.

The schools involved in the TVEI Pilot Schemes have found the appointment of a specialist school co-ordinator a *sine qua non*. The need to support curriculum development at a detailed level, liaise with the Training Agency, LEA, examining boards and other agencies, administer financial systems and cohort records and, most importantly, talk to pupils, parents and colleagues are tasks which no headteacher could sustain alone. Arguably all secondments which lead to changing practice in schools need such a framework of support. Unless external funding such as TVEI Extension schemes are available most schools cannot afford such necessities.

Another group which has had considerable impact on schools are the two hundred probationers who were appointed to replace the seconded teachers in 1986. Having gone through a long period when it had only been possible to appoint very few probationers, some secondary schools found themselves with five 'new' teachers bringing enthusiasm and new ideas into the school. Many proved to be excellent and, in some cases, their ideas have become integrated into practice. For example, one school developed new approaches to more able pupils as a result of input from a probationer. However, the appointments were made to the authority not the individual schools and at the end of the school year the reduction in numbers to be seconded the following year, brought about by the ending of the pooling system and the cuts in the INSET budget, meant many probationers had to be redeployed. This was often a matter of considerable disappointment to all concerned. It is, however, interesting to record that in the Summer term of 1989 two of the probationers are themselves to be seconded to the SFD programme.

In many cases the secondment of teachers has made possible the temporary promotion of others to fill their jobs for the year. This has also proved a developmental process and in some cases has opened up the possibility of thinking more creatively about posts of responsibility in schools and the career development of teachers. Once again these positive developments occur concurrently with cutbacks and reductions. There is some concern that the skills of staff are being rapidly developed and their aspirations raised at a time when the job market is closing down and their chances of promotion are being severely reduced.

A recent consequence of the falling birth rate has been in one case the closure, and in six cases the amalgamation of secondary schools (primary schools having experienced this situation earlier). Amalgamation is a stressful time particularly because so many redeployments are involved. It is important to try and find a positive response. For example, although the situation is undeniably difficult, it provides an opportunity to reconsider the way the school is structured and the lengthy counselling procedures set up in schools by the authority has enabled at least some teachers to think more carefully about their strengths and their career possibilities.

Other staff are inevitably affected by all of the above. Where commissions have been carefully negotiated and staff involved and committed to the developments, the effects on teaching have been widest spread. In general we have been aware of a sense of opening up, of barriers between departments being lowered, or even removed, of greater mutual understanding developing across schools. The process of drawing up, then carrying out, school commissions has ensured that in-depth discussion of the curriculum is taking place in a way that we have not experienced before. In some cases a more sophisticated understanding of curriculum issues has been picked up by outsiders, including HMI. This is of course not a painless process. Once the curriculum and its supporting structure are up for review there is bound to be difference of opinion and the debate can be quite fierce at times. However, the discussion, the examination of practice and the sharing of experiences develops understanding of the philosophy and values that underpin what we do and is ultimately a unifying process.

Pupils and the Curriculum

Underpinning the variety of developments generated through SCI (and hopefully all of what happens in schools) is the intention to improve the quality of what is offered to pupils, to change their experience of learning for the better. It is essential to focus on this purpose and we must constantly ask ourselves whether this is happening, if not, what is preventing it happening and what is going to be done about it.

Some of the changes introduced in schools are highly visible and involve changes to the organization and structure. For example, in schools involved in the TVEI initiative, all fourth and fifth year pupils now take part in an 80 per cent core entitlement curriculum with 20 per cent options in contrast to the 40 per cent core, 60 per cent option programme that preceded this development. Several secondary schools have introduced radical changes to the arrangements for the first year of secondary schooling. These have, most commonly, focused on the development of integrated curriculum areas such as creative arts, humanities, maths and science, or balanced science – and by reducing the number of staff teaching the first years. In two secondaries in the city 'mini schools' have been introduced.

Changes of this magnitude have not been undertaken without considerable thought and reflection. A good deal of attention has been paid to examining the pupils' experience of schooling. Information has been collected through such activities as tracking pupils through their school day, pupil interviews and classroom observations in both secondary and primary schools. In many cases the thinking predates the SCI initiative. Some of the changes that are being introduced were discussed in a series of conferences between advisers and headteachers over a four-year period which resulted in a *Patterns and Processes* paper in 1982, and several schools had formed working parties to explore these ideas further. Some developments had been held up by the 'teacher action' in the mid-eighties and the secondment programmes provided a new impetus as well as the vital element of time which is normally at such a premium in schools.

However, schools have to respond not only to LEA initiatives but also to those emanating from central government. Having coped with the introduction of GCSE, despite the well documented difficulties, primary and secondary schools are now preparing to cope with the ERA. As yet, in the Spring term 1989, we do not know in any detail how the National Curriculum will affect our schools. There are clearly implications for pupils. There is concern that there will be pressure to abandon any integrated approaches to the curriculum and that there may be a threat to the mixed ability teaching that exists in our schools with a temptation to retreat to the convenience (for teachers) of streaming. It is not yet clear how constraining the regular testing will be

on what can be offered to pupils nor of the consequences for their
self-esteem. There is a very real possibility that the amount of positive
collaboration between schools within the authority will be at risk in a
climate where we are going to have to compete for a diminishing
number of pupils because of the falling rolls.

Thus other changes that are occurring both nationally and locally
are affecting schools. The fall in the birth rate, which is particularly
dramatic in Sheffield, is currently affecting secondary schools, coinciding with the cutbacks in spending and having considerable effect. Not
all new developments cost money. However, it is not possible to
produce new materials and resources without money or without the
non-teaching staff whose back up is essential. It is difficult, for example,
for a school to introduce balanced science at a time where their
laboratory assistants are being cut from three to one. It is unfortunate
that the delivery phase of the initiative is coinciding with a downswing
in educational funding. Ten years ago things might have been very
different.

Developments that are less easy to define and more difficult to enact
are also taking place in the classrooms encouraged by the SCI initiative.
Changes in teaching style that enable more active and experiential
learning (perhaps most particularly in secondary schools) group work,
negotiation with pupils and enabling and encouraging pupil self-
assessment may require considerable personal change in teaching style
and approach. There is also a more flexible approach to timetabling
with different lesson lengths being tried out or particular curriculum
areas being timetabled together so as to facilitate cross-curricular links
where appropriate. Some secondees have contributed a good deal of
time and effort to these issues, sometimes coming back into the
classroom with their approach to these matters 'transformed' by their
experience on secondment. Groups of staff and where possible, through
the use of Curriculum Days, whole staffs have been involved in INSET
activities in many schools around these themes.

No school has experienced secondments on this scale before,
particularly secondments of this pro-active kind. We have had nowhere
to look for 'good practice' to emulate and we, and those who have been
supporting us, have had to learn as we go along. Despite the many
benefits there have been some negative consequences for pupils particularly when teachers have been out of the classroom on short-term
release connected with the various developments in schools. There has
been some debate about the 'best' secondment pattern. Year-long

secondments minimize disruption for pupils and maximize the benefits for individual teachers, but only a small number of teachers can be involved. The CDI project opted to second fifteen teachers in each of the four schools involved on a rolling programme which involved them in spending a term out of the classroom, a term in to try out new ideas and then further time out for reflection. The balance between the costs of 'time out' for teachers to reflect on their practice and develop new approaches has at all times to be carefully weighed against the undoubted benefits. Whatever the secondment pattern, inevitably it will take time for the new approaches to permeate all teachers and all corners of a school. We may have to think in terms of five or even ten years before these changes can be firmly established.

There are, however, already hopeful signs. For example, 'continuity' provided a unifying focus for the commissions of the primary secondees 1987/8, each school choosing the precise area in which to work on this theme. The time available to the secondee in one school enabled her, among other things, to spend time working alongside her colleagues in every classroom in the school. This experience highlighted the fact that although the staff worked well together and believed they shared many common aims and similar practices this was not really so. Classroom practice and the underpinning philosophy actually varied considerably. This insight provided the impetus for the whole staff to address their differences and to work together with the intention of reducing them to ensure more coherence and less confusion for pupils, but not a restraining uniformity. This experience has also encouraged staff to feel more united and more confident about facing the introduction of the National Curriculum to 5-year olds in September 1989.

A strategy employed by an increasing number of secondary schools has been the creative use of 'suspended timetable' events. For example, a two day Arts Festival in one school brought in 150 'artists' including painters, sculptors, woodcarvers and musicians to work with the pupils. There is increasing interest in raising pupils' consciousness of what and how they are learning. The introduction of modularization and unit accreditation has had considerable effect here as this approach encourages teachers to ensure that pupils understand and can explain what exactly they have achieved and how and when this achievement came about. Pupil involvement in self-assessment through Records of Achievement and Experience also furthers such developments. The understanding of the pupil experience that teachers gain through such activities in its turn influences how they plan future lessons.

Parents and Governors

The degree to which parents and governors have been involved in what is happening varies considerably from school to school. In some schools, both secondary and primary, parental and/or community links have been the focus of school commissions. In others, changes to areas such as fourth-year options or work on transition from one stage of education to another has directly involved parents. In all schools governors have been kept informed and, to varying degrees, involved in what has been happening. The new legislation affecting governors is not resulting in a uniform response. For example, in at least one secondary school, governors are expressing a desire to be involved in all decisions on staffing, whilst in a neighbouring school they wish to delegate responsibility for all posts below that of deputy, to the head.

Where parents have been involved and consulted about SCI developments the response has been generally positive, although there are always some difficulties when a school wishes to change the status quo. For example, in a school involved in the TVEI initiative many parents were worried about the move from a 40 per cent core/60 per cent optional curriculum to 80 per cent core/20 per cent option. In this situation the introduction of the National Curriculum has proved to be a helpful intervention. Some parents also expressed concern about the movement away from the separate subjects that they had experienced (or opted out of) during their own schooling into unfamiliar areas such as 'balanced science' or 'integrated humanities'. The head and staff learned very quickly that the way in which the issue was introduced to parents and the language that was used was absolutely critical. For example, if parents were asked what kind of basic grounding in science they would like their children to have, their responses were, almost invariably, remarkably similar to the new balanced science curriculum.

One school found that the prospect of equal opportunities was not welcomed by all parents, some of whom initially resisted some proposals, for example, there was some questioning of the requirement that all pupils should study information technology. Some parents felt that this was inappropriate for girls or that boys should not need keyboard skills. However, work within the school and more general influences within society have influenced such reservations and the school has found that over three years this resistance has disappeared.

Learning how best to work with and consult parents always provides a challenge for schools. Even in a primary school with an apparently homogeneous catchment area there is unlikely to be one unanimous view on any aspect of the curriculum or any educational philosophy. Parents can also be influenced by comments in the media about what is allegedly happening in schools. It is not unknown for a head to be faced by a parent waving a critical cutting from a national newspaper. We have found that these occasions are best seen as an opportunity for some lively debate and a chance to explain one's own school's philosophy and approach.

In a primary school the interviews with parents carried out by the SFD secondee generated staff discussion over a period of several months. From this came a perceptible improvement in the relationship between parents and children. More positive attitudes became apparent in staff meetings, parents' assemblies were welcomed and a detailed document of the school's policy on parental involvement was drawn up. This outlined, among other things, the ways in which parents can work alongside teachers in the classroom. The school expects to make more progress in this area and is particularly interested in considering ways of keeping touch with parent opinion on a wide variety of issues. Relationships with parents, always on important issue, is even more so in a climate in which we see parents being given misleading information about 'what is wrong with schools' in general, that can cause difficulties if they are out of touch with what is really happening in their child's school.

Organization/Management and Structural Change

We have referred at several points in this chapter to the effects of what has been taking place on the way that schools are managed. Sometimes this effect is on the actual structure and at others on the process of working together. A paragraph from a paper on *Managing Curriculum Development* drawn up after wide discussion with staff in one school and distributed as the prelude to further deliberation summarizes many of the issues:-

> Inevitably curriculum development has not yet managed to include all staff. In addition curriculum areas/departments are working at different speeds and sometimes in different direc-tions. A number of schemes are being put forward as potential pilot schemes for next year. How do we decide which should go ahead? How do we communicate effectively what is happening throughout the school and get everyone involved to some

extent in the decision making processes? It is vital that we develop a decision-making structure which can cope with new initiatives, whilst developing a whole school perspective, effective evaluation, communication and high levels of participation.

It is always necessary to hold the balance between openness to new possibilities and coherence across the whole school.

This school places a high value on participation and there is a general and growing recognition across the authority that a clearly defined consultation process is an essential feature of any initiative. Working parties and interest groups can be useful if other staff are kept informed and the dangers of becoming a clique are avoided. More open and participative staff and departmental meetings, sometimes facilitated by secondees and others rather than senior management, are enabling even less confident members of staff to contribute to discussions.

In an increasing number of schools it is recognised that non-teaching staff should also be involved in decision making. The school above involved all its non-teaching staff in a residential training experience during which the school's Framework for Action was drawn up. The School Registrar is a permanent member of the senior management team and is chairing the school's finance group thus further demonstrating a commitment to value all members of staff equally. Access to the senior team is considered to be part of this school's staff development policy. The staff were asked if they would like to be attached to the team temporarily. So far four teachers have responded to this offer and as a consequence have joined the team, two at a time, for one term. The whole management team welcome this development wholeheartedly and the teachers are 'full voting' members whose contributions to the discussions are valued.

In general a good deal of attention is being paid to the issue of staff development in schools. Secondment and temporary promotions are developmental but it is important that other staff that are not involved do not feel left out or disadvantaged. If teachers are being asked to change their practice they must be offered the necessary support. It is essential to maintain and if possible raise morale. However there are many factors with which to contend. The enforced nature of the ERA, the implicit (or even explicit) devaluing of professional expertise, the pace at which the changes are to be introduced and the possibility that some of its elements may cut across carefully researched developments in school are not conducive to positive thinking. In addition, the cuts in staffing, the new salary structures and conditions of service that are coinciding with falling rolls (resulting in smaller schools) often make it impossible to provide new allowances for new jobs. If senior staff leave they may have to be replaced by someone on a lower allowance. In the worst case, it may not be possible to replace them at all.

This can cause difficulties, perhaps most particularly in secondary schools which have tended to be organized and managed through a subject-based, departmental structure often with a pastoral care structure running alongside, but in many ways separate, within the school. However, the focus on the pupils' experience of learning and what is happening in the classroom is leading to increasing acceptance that children's needs cannot be divided into those that are pastoral, academic and administrative. This understanding is leading to the collapsing of the pastoral/academic divide and the building of new cross curriculum responsibilities, for example, special needs and technology across the curriculum which may require new appointments. One advantage of the removal of this divide is that more creative thinking about the role of deputy heads becomes possible.

Involvement in SFD, CDI or TVEI have all involved schools in committing longer term plans to paper. In some ways this has been a helpful exercise and has made public, to those both in and out of schools, the thinking that is taking place. However, when the carrying out of projected plans has been closely tied to continuing funding, as in the case of TVEI, it can be more problematical. Sometimes the pressure to meet targets on time has meant changes taking place at a pace that allows for little flexibility and sensitivity. Whilst it is helpful to have a 'mission plan' and a shared sense of purpose, some systems maintenance and some 'security zones' are also necessary. We are aware that once caught up in a process, staff can make tremendous demands on themselves and that we have a part to play in reducing the pressure where possible.

Recognition of the need for co-ordinated planning for curriculum change includes understanding of the importance of planned, on-going, formative evaluation. It is essential that this process is built in from the beginning rather than tacked on at the end when it is too late to influence practice. Some schools have set up evaluation groups involving secondees or made evaluation the focus of a commission. The activities described earlier such as interviewing pupils, teachers and parents, pupil-tracking and classroom observation are not only offering illumination of the pupils' experience but also enabling teachers to become more articulate about what they are doing and why. An increasing number of teachers are carrying out evaluation of their own practice and developing the confidence to open their classroom to colleagues with whom findings can be shared. These demanding activities are increasing the motivation among staff to discuss what is happening in classrooms, demonstrated by requests for meetings in which these discussions can take place.

As part of SCI, the LEA has introduced a new organizational feature, that of secondary 'clusters', which link, on an area basis, comprehensive and special secondary schools and the new tertiary colleges into groups of about six to eight institutions. Meetings take place as each cluster decides, usually at least every four to six weeks, and are also attended by LEA officers and advisers, members of the SFD and CAR teams and careers officers. Clusters are said to be designed to create more 'human sized' groups than the authority-wide secondary heads' meetings in which representatives of the schools and the LEA can discuss issues together. This arrangement has met with a somewhat mixed reception by heads, some finding them very useful and supportive, whilst others suspected a 'bureaucratic device' or would have preferred clusters to have been established on other than an area basis. Although primary schools do not take part in these cluster meetings, when it is appropriate, primary INSET is increasingly organized on a pyramid/cluster basis as is any joint primary/secondary activity. The clusters have now been identified as the 'Consortia' required by the Training Agency for TVEI Extension and this has given them new impetus.

This is particularly true for the clusters that have been selected to bid for the first phase of TVEI Extension. Each of these two clusters used a Curriculum day in January 1989 to organize a cross-cluster event, one focusing on Records of Achievement and Experience and the other an opportunity for teachers to get together in cross-school groups to discuss the implications of the bid and consider future action. In both cases this meant the bringing together of approximately 350 teachers in subject/curriculum area and interest groups to share experiences and forming links which are now being extended. The RAE sub-group in one of these clusters also meets regularly with its primary feeder schools to discuss the development of an RAE from 3–16.

The Effects on Headteachers

Many of the issues we have described in this chapter have direct implications for heads. For years there has been a movement, in

Sheffield as elsewhere, away from an autocratic, 'top down' style of management to one that is collaborative and consultative. This approach has been encouraged by such activities as Schools Curriculum Industry Partnership, SCIP and management conferences, but springs as much from heads' own recognition that not only are autocratically imposed decisions unlikely to be effective (much energy being used to undermine them) but also that they are inappropriate between professionals.

The relationship between heads and their deputies is in many schools a close and supportive one, giving real meaning to the term Senior Management *Team* but collaboration should not be confined to this area. A management style does not depend entirely on the attitude of the head, however. If the school culture has for years been one in which everyone expects the head to manage and everyone else to grumble it may be difficult to persuade some staff to take on the responsibility that is being shared. Even in the most participative school it is not unknown, in moments of tiredness and irritation, for staff to say 'It's your job to manage. Get on and manage', and not all parents welcome a more approachable, friendly and consultative head, some seeming to prefer the authority figures from their past. It is important for everyone to reflect on the difference between such concepts as 'consultation', 'decision-making', 'delegation' and that of 'abrogating responsibility'.

As we have said earlier, an open and clear-cut process of consultation is critical; this should include agreement on how necessary decisions are to be made. Complete consensus is not possible on all issues. If a minority of staff are unhappy about a decision there is a shared responsibility to minimize damage. We can look for 'win win' situations but must have the resources to respond if a member of staff feels that she or he has lost out over some issue. A headteacher's visible demonstration of valuing all members of staff, even when not sharing a particular viewpoint, has considerable symbolic importance.

When tasks are delegated it is essential that it is agreed what has been delegated, that help is available if needed and how much should be reported back, by when and to whom. If such agreement is reached it must be adhered to. Apparent delegation that is followed by constant checking-up and interference is probably at least as damaging as no delegation at all. It is also not enough for heads to talk about their 'accessibility'; it needs to be demonstrated. Many heads now make a point of saying, and meaning, 'My door is always open', even if this means that the paper work is done after the school day is ended.

Another area in which the head's support is essential, is that of resource allocation. As we have said, curriculum development may not always cost money but on many occasions there is a genuine need. A headteacher can alert governing bodies and financial/capitation committees to the impending need. Financial management can then take account of the situation, respond if possible and therefore enhance the outcome of a secondment. The likelihood of secondees becoming depressed or cynical because of the inability of the budget to meet the demands is reduced. The setting up of representative finance committees in schools in which priorities are discussed and decisions openly made are another demonstration of a change of management style. Heads have a part to play but no longer use capitation as a form of patronage within the school. We are also concerned about the impact of the ERA in this context and are worried that we may be pulled further into spending time on financial management and away from pupils and the curriculum.

A strategy that has traditionally been used by some heads to keep control is that of claiming the sole right to having an overview of what is happening in a school, 'if you knew what I know ...'. We would not wish to take this stance but are aware that there must be coherence and balance within a school. Opening up channels of communication, sharing information and making sure that 'what we know' is available to other staff, helps decision-making and increases commitment to carrying out any action that is agreed. The fact that new ideas are being brought into schools by 'ordinary' teachers can increase commitment in a way that may be more difficult for a head to generate.

We must admit that there are moments of doubt, that there are times when we feel that things are going on that we are not a party to, that the energy that has been released is somehow passing us by. However, heads must resist any temptation to move in, take over and direct. We know that a return to the days when ideas and strategies were the exclusive property of senior management would mean that both we and our schools would be the poorer. There are few, if any, right or wrong answers about how to manage the complex human organization that is a school. We cannot resort to tossing a coin to decide on a solution. Apart from the fact that (as our title implies) any decision-making coin would need at least ten sides to cover the available options, we know that the only lasting decisions are those that involve others. Heads have a real responsibility for what happens and this is by no means diminished by being shared.

Conclusion

The rate of change facing schools shows no sign of slowing, with the ERA affecting the management of schools (and therefore, inevitably, the role of the head) in many ways. There will be a whole new relationship with the LEA which has as yet to be fully understood and accepted on both sides. In April 1989, the focus of the Sheffield regular, annual, residential, two day conference for secondary heads and LEA officers and advisers was this new relationship. As we grappled with the volume and nature of the pending changes it became clear that there was a shared sense of purpose amongst all concerned that we did not wish to lose. Whilst it was possible to welcome a considerable degree of decentralization, fragmentation of the service was a different matter. There was agreement on the need for co-operation and collaboration, that schools and teachers benefit from working together and sharing both their ideas and city-wide resources. There was a shared vision that schools and teachers best serve their particular students and communities when they are also aware of the city, national and global context. It was recognized that co-operation and collaboration do not, and should not, preclude a diversity of local provision. Addressing the vexed issue of consultation, there was a commitment to set out the ground rules, to identify all those who should be involved and to agree the process through which decisions will be reached. Concern was voiced as to how the old structures would adapt to give way to the new, and acceptance that time and opportunity must be found to enable all these issues to be thoroughly addressed.

Overall, there was a determination to found a new partnership between schools, the LEA, parents, the community and politicians to ensure the delivery of a quality service to all children and young people in the city. This is our shared task for the future.

The schools:

Handsworth Grange Secondary
Herries Secondary
Gleadless Valley Secondary
Sir Harold Jackson Junior/Infant
Wisewood Secondary.

Part Three
Some Wider Perspectives

7
A View from West Germany

Fritz Bohnsack

Introduction

The 'view from West Germany' can have advantages and disadvantages. As author of this chapter, I was in close contact with the Sheffield Curriculum Initiative from October 1988 to January 1989. In spite of this long period of observation, I could not gain the same accumulated knowledge and insight as the reformers themselves, and there may remain some misunderstandings. On the other hand there were and are certain possibilities for me as a foreigner to see things from a distance and differently: because of my diverse educational background, experiences and concepts of what schools and INSET are or should be, I may perhaps see the Sheffield Curriculum Initiative from a different perspective.

As a basis of my report I shall use: my own observations visiting schools and participating in the School-Focused Development programme, talks to teachers and tutors and to university staff, my own interviews with secondees and other teachers and the mimeographed or printed reports of the Sheffield colleagues. As my interest is more a systematic then a historic one, I shall use reports of all three years, 1986–89, without stressing developments during the earlier period of SFS/SFD.

Any evaluation requires values: one cannot evaluate without a set of criteria. Firstly, I shall develop these from the present national and global situations and the corresponding tasks of schools, as seen from West German experience and comparing them with British experiences. Secondly, I shall try to analyze the general aims and structures of the Sheffield Curriculum Initiative. Thirdly, I shall give an evaluation of the Initiative's success.

Fritz Bohnsack

Criteria for Evaluation: The Tasks of Schools Facing Changes in Society and Youth

The following argument tries to develop criteria for evaluation by integrating traditional educational aims with new tasks of the schools derived from 'objective' changes in society and the global scene, and 'subjective' changes in the values and attitudes of learners.

Education for Democracy

Investigations into the 'hidden curriculum' have proved that the effects of schooling, at least partly, are anti-educational and anti-democratic. At the Conference of the International Study Association on Teacher Thinking (ISATT) at Nottingham (September, 1988), a Canadian colleague called the training of obedience, submission and uncritical judgments enforced by the usual teaching methods: 'fascist'. Schools have not shed the pre-democratic structures of the nineteenth century, neither in their interactional (teacher-pupil relations) and method-ological (teaching methods) practices, nor the hierarchical dependencies within their staff, management and administration. One criterion for good schools today, therefore, is the degree to which they succeed in realizing participation and self-responsibility amongst staff and students: how far they achieve a planned and long-term education of the students' growing responsibility for their own development. In other words: the judgment on the success of in-service training and school reform has to look for the realization of education (Bildung) in the classical sense of the term. A German colleague recently defined this as capability of self-determination, participation and solidarity (Klafki, 1985).

Education for Global Responsibility – Value Changes in Society and Youth

Schools in Britain and West Germany have very different historical backgrounds (e.g. autonomy of local authorities and of individual schools vs. central or state administration). Nevertheless, similar indus-trial and social developments and global threats have created similar problems in schools and changes in their responsibilities. Wolfgang Klafki tries to 'update' the classical concept of 'Bildung' by reconciling or integrating it with urgent tasks of our present time; the education for peace (atomic threat), rescue of the environment, the problems of unemployment, the Third World, etc. The present discussion of environmental destruction has shown that the cure is not effected merely by reducing the pollution of air and water, but demands a rather radical change of our thinking and treating nature as raw material for human (and in-human) purposes and progress. The implications of this change which touch the very principles of science and technology as well as the aims and structures of school subjects and teaching, are far from being understood and developed in schools. Teachers in many parts of the world have started developing methods and materials for lessons with a world-wide perspective. A British example of this sort of work is the Centre for Global Education at the University of York which has published a series of teaching/learning resources such as the illustrated teacher's handbook 'Earthrights: Education as if the planet really mattered' (Greig *et al.*, 1987) or the manual 'Global Teacher, Global Learner' (Pike *et al.*, 1987) which – based on work and experience with teachers in twenty-two LEAs – comprises global issues of subjects such as mathematics, methods like exercises in feedback and evaluation techniques with student groups, changes in the teacher's role as well as implications for teacher education and INSET. Eduard Werner Kleber gives an account of the West German Literature in this area, (Kleber, 1985).

The educational importance of the changes towards democracy and towards global responsibility is related to that of other value transformation in society. Helmut Klages (1985) summarizes German findings by describing a general retreat of 'values of duty and acceptance' (Pflicht und Akzeptanzwerte) such as obedience, subordination, order and discipline, and an advance of 'values of self-development' (Selbstentfaltungswerte) such as creativity, spontaneity, autonomy and independent responsibility. According to empirical research, these changes are more prominent with younger (aged 18–28 years) and better educated people. These general social movements are connected with particular developments in young people such as more widespread membership of peer groups (1962, 16.2 per cent; 1983, 56.9 per cent) accompanied by a move of socializing influences from adults to peers, by earlier sexual relationships and by a corresponding change of moral views: these youngsters experience aspects of adult life, yet whilst in school they are treated as children (see Allerbeck *et al.*, 1985; Hurrelmann *et al.*, 1985; Fischer *et al.*, 1982; Klages, 1985).

Another aspect is their scepticism about the future, caused by professional (unemployment) and global (environmental destruction, etc.) uncertainties and their desire to experience fulfilment in the present. This, according to Klages does not imply that young people are generally less ready to make efforts and achieve. Teachers, however, find it more difficult to stimulate these efforts and provide the conditions for them within the institutional structures of the schools. Klages differentiates between a traditional type of readiness and ability to make efforts which may be defined as a disposition to hard work caused by outside demands and aims, from a new type which is initiated and controlled by individual motivation and which is stimulated and driven by the desire for realizing personal interests, needs, abilities and ideas of fulfilment or significance.

Concepts of a 'Good' School and of the In-service Training of Teachers

As far as pay, teaching load and public esteem are concerned, teachers in West Germany are better off then their colleagues in Britain. What they are dissatisfied with, if not suffering from, is the teaching situation in the classroom. Because of the value changes I have indicated, students are increasingly unable or unwilling to accept unpleasant or alienating features of schooling which they still tolerated one or two decades ago. They experience schools as places where they are excluded from decision-making and the sort of self-determination which they have outside: they do not feel to be 'owners' of themselves and they develop an inner distance from what schools have to offer. They avoid engagement which is a precondition of real education whilst school and teachers struggle to stop and reverse this loss of educational motivation.

It is impossible here to outline the concepts and structures of a 'good' school which have been developed recently by empirical research and educational theory (summaries in Haenisch, 1986, Steffens, 1986; see also Ermert, 1987, Steffens *et al.*, 1987/88). For example, they point to the necessity of improved co-operation of staff, of effective but more democratic school management, more student-centred teaching methods and styles, a better school 'climate', and closer co-operation with parents. Educational theorists as well as teachers call attention to the importance of treating students as persons increasingly responsible for their own development and no longer as objects to be filled with knowledge: they conceptualize the idea of a really democratic school and its implications for the act of teaching.

According to these concepts and the projects and experiments trying to realize them, there can be no doubt that the students' 'ownership' of their learning demands the teachers' 'ownership' of school reform; or that student-centred learning has to be prepared, facilitated and introduced by participant-centred in-service training. Any other more authoritarian method would – by its means – prevent the realization of the aims.

Aims and General Structures of the Sheffield Curriculum Initiative

The Aims of the Initiative

In the preceding paragraphs I tried to outline some central goals of school reform in our time. In the following sections I shall apply these criteria to the aims and realization of the Sheffield Curriculum Initiative: how far do these correspond to the needs for:

— an education for democracy, e.g. for critical judgment, self-determination, participation and solidarity;
— a 'global' education for peace and rescue of the environment as well as other urgent social problems;
— a treatment of students as 'persons' with a growing self-responsibility and say in matters of their own learning, experiencing the schools' offer as significant for their own present life and development.

A view of the Chief Education Officer's letter of December 1985 (reprinted earlier in this volume) or the LEA's pamphlet 'Curriculum Policy' (1988) or the collection of reports about the beginning of the reform edited by Jon Nixon (1987) shows that Sheffield schools are, indeed, expected to achieve a 'radical change in what is offered to children',

— by increasing democratic structures in schools;
— by developing elements of self-determination and participation of students;
— by making subject matter more vital and significant;

— by strengthening student-centred teaching methods as well as
active and experiential learning;
— by fostering 'equal opportunities' for all.

This last aspect corresponds to Klafki's aim of solidarity mentioned
previously. The whole network of reform aims seem to answer the
necessities I have pointed out before and would address the global
perspective without problems, although it is not referred to explicitly.

The General Structures of the Reform

If in-service training intends the students' 'ownership' of learning, it
must make possible the teachers' 'ownership' of the reform. This has
been the declared principle of the Sheffield approach. But the problem
of how to reconcile the realization of a local authority's (or edu-
cationalist's) vision of a better or 'good' school with the autonomy of
teachers remains critical and partly unsolved, in the British as well as
international scene.

Reviewing international, especially US research findings, Ray
Bolam *et al.*, 1985, have listed the main features of effective professional
development (in Hopkins, 1985). They report:

1 that school-based INSET was more effective in changing
   complex behaviour and teacher attitudes than short or long
   courses outside of school;
2 that 'collaborative planning' between school staff and
   authorities was more successful than either 'top-down' or
   'grass-roots' (without outside help) approaches;
3 that more fundamental changes demand 'conceptual clarity',
   which has to be provided, not at the 'front-end' but as a process
   during implementation;
4 that reforming schools means changing of persons and roles as
   well as of organizational structures, e.g. 'authority relationships, communication networks, status groupings, and
   even friendship cliques;
5 that this implies assessing, diagnosing and transforming by staff
   members themselves, though with the help of outside consultants;
6 that the commonly held structure of values and expectations of

staff make them resist innovations but, if appropriately tackled, also may offer a 'tool for planned change';

7 that staff have to learn strategies of clarifying group relations, improving communications, establishing common goals, solving problems and conflicts, making decisions and assessing progress of change;

8 that consultants or tutors need to be organized officially as a group or 'formal sub-system' with a budget at their disposal (as in the Sheffield SFD programme by the tutorial team);

9 and that they need to be trained in group dynamics, using brainstorming, role-play, feedback, simulations, etc.

I shall use these criteria in evaluating the Sheffield programme. Ray Bolam *et al.*, (1985), distinguish between 'fine tuning' existing approaches by consolidation of competence and increase of effectiveness, and mastering new approaches (such as in the Sheffield reform) which require an understanding of 'rationale' or theory, a learning of new strategies, a command of new content – altogether a much more complex and difficult task. The empirical findings seem to show that the latter, with 'progress to the transfer level' is only accomplished by a *combination* of:

— presentation of theory which raises awareness and increased conceptional control;
— demonstration of unfamiliar models of teaching;
— practice under simulated conditions (with peers or small groups of students);
— regular and consistent feedback;
— on-site coaching to application.

The following sections will answer the question how far these procedures have been practiced in Sheffield. Whereas in the formulation of Bolam *et al.*, they have retained a certain 'formal' diction, leaving final aims or structures of a 'good' school fairly open, the Sheffield Initiative from its very beginning has worked within a relatively clear framework of general intentions and goals. I think this is a pre-condition of success, if, at the same time, the initiators foster the 'ownership' of the application and detailed interpretation of their 'vision' according to particular school contexts.

This is not necessarily a contradiction, as outside direction – in a 'dialectic' way transcending this contra – need not mean reduction of autonomy but can adopt the character of facilitating it. As far as I can see, this has been the case in Sheffield: The authority's priorities were not handed out 'top-down' as a 'blue-print', but negotiated as a 'sense of direction' (Aspinwall, 1987d, 1989) which left the substance of commissions and the pace and extent of development to the conditions and decisions of the individual school.

The term 'school-based' brings the Sheffield reform into the wider context of similar projects in Britain and abroad. 'School-*focused*' indicates a difference. School-based INSET in a narrower sense of the term usually means the workings of consultants with a group of teachers or a whole staff, who volunteer to take part. The LEA in Sheffield wanted *all* their secondary schools (and some primary) to participate. So they could not leave the participation open to the majority vote of each school's staff. Against the present background international discussion of effectiveness of INSET and the claims of school-based approaches to be more effective we shall have to ask to what degree the Sheffield reform has reached the whole staff in schools.

The Sheffield Curriculum Initiative has tried to avoid the 'dangers of insularity and lack of challenge' sometimes connected with merely school-based procedures (Aspinwall, 1989), by merging elements of the latter with those of a school-focused approach which, at least partly, has the character of outside courses led by the tutor team. The secondees experience this combination of more academic, though school-related, theory and its application, the 'continuous rhythm of the inside/outside process' (Aspinwall, 1987a) as a tension which disturbs everyday routines of practice and thinking, as well as stimulating creativity, an effect probably not possible in totally school-based or totally out-of-school courses.

In other words: the Sheffield approach supplies two levels of facilitating innovations in schools, namely by the tutors who support secondees, and by the secondees who encourage their colleagues in school. At the same time, each tutor keeps close contact with a cluster of schools, supervises the progress of the secondees' commissions and tries to foster innovation through communication with staff, senior management and heads. Insofar he/she fulfils demands of Bolam *et al.*, mentioned above. Many of these colleagues express their appreciation of 'their' tutor's work in school, some are enthusiastic about it. Both tutors and secondees have to find the delicate and narrow path between response to immediate needs, which might leave the school in a limited definition of change, and the imposition of alienating aims (Aspinwall,

1987d). A correct balance between these poles or even conflicting demands represents an important criterion of 'success' in terms of staff involvement in change.

Only somebody unfamiliar with two decades of innovation research can expect that all the schools and all teachers would be won over to the reform without resistance. Change in schools means change in people. Changing oneself causes anxieties and resistance. The aim of whole staff change, therefore is a far reaching one and requires several years of preparation and progress.

This means that common goals are a condition of effective innovation and, vice versa, change is a way of achieving this sort of communality. Accordingly, though supported by the authority, secondees in all schools met some colleagues unwilling to take part in this initiative, sometimes because they were overburdened with other innovations (GCSE, tertiary reorganization, school amalgamation, ERA, etc), sometimes because of more personal attitudes such as preferring 'traditional views' to changing the 'status quo', scepticism about the success or simply complacency (Aspinwall, 1988a). In schools with strong academic traditions and departmental structures staff had greater problems in identifying themselves with whole school issues: e.g. they were afraid of dissolution of subjects by integrated curricula in the lower school, later loss of A-level candidates, or resistance of parents (Fulker *et al.*, 1987). In the beginning parents and the wider community were often not sufficiently informed or involved.

So secondees, in their reform enthusiasm of the first year, in some cases feeling like 'revolutionaries' or even 'missionaries' and 'crusaders', had to learn ways of 'delicate handling' of colleagues to avoid their resistance, ways of not 'dragging' them but facilitating changes they wanted to achieve themselves (Nixon, 1987; Aspinwall, 1989; Rudduck and Wilcox, 1988).

Although most headteachers accepted the framework of the reform policy as in line with their own ideas (Rudduck and Wilcox, 1988), their habits of management sometimes produced problems. They consulted senior management and some individual teachers about the school's commission and the selection of secondees but the whole staff was not necessarily involved in the decision-making process. Few heads used whole school review approaches such as the GRIDS (SCDC, 1986) material to survey staff opinion instead of informal consultation (Fulker *et al.*, 1987). In these cases an opportunity of developing a focus for the whole school was not used.

In some schools the commissions were regarded and welcomed as 'natural choice', especially if they continued existing projects, some-times backed by public opinion. In these cases it was helpful if secondees informed their colleagues by meeting them in small groups or tutorials and not merely by written handouts and displays on notice boards. The chance of successful implementation was increased by open-minded school co-ordinators who were able to bridge the gap between secondees and staff 'feeding information back and forth and constantly monitoring feelings and perceptions'. Often there was little time for team teaching by teachers and secondees, for observing one another, i.e. for common planning and lesson reviews (Fulker *et al.*, 1987; Aspinwall, 1988c).

Another respect of this problem is the – internationally well-known – re-entry difficulty at the end of secondments. Sometimes the structures of the schools forced secondees to slip back into old habits and see their intentions fail (Aspinwall, 1989). In many cases head-teachers and senior management did not find ways of sustaining the engagement of secondees, of reintegrating them and helping them keep contact with the team of the following year. These re-entry problems seem to have been reduced to the extent that secondees succeed in conveying a feeling of 'ownership' and shared responsibility for innovations to their colleagues.

On the other hand the re-entry dilemma, I take it, is an indication of the differences between school-based INSET in the narrower sense and the Sheffield school-focused approach: it is the price to be paid for the opportunity and privilege to step back, view from the outside and develop more open and critical reflection.

Some Remarks on the 'Success' of the Sheffield Curriculum Initiative

The question of whether the Sheffield Initiative has been successful or not requires a differentiated answer. The answer does not only depend on the expectations or criteria of the evaluator. It has to take into account that any organisation development is a long-term process. Knowing that the desired radical changes in their schools demand teachers' 'ownership' of the necessary innovations, the Sheffield Authority has planned for and envisaged a long-term development. So the above question rather boils down to asking whether the changes are in the right direction in terms of the aims of a 'good' school outlined previously and whether they could have been more effective in the first two and a half years of the Initiative. My general response to these questions is positive, but I would like to distinguish between personal, staff and institutional effects.

With very few exceptions all secondees in retrospect expressed an appreciation of their development, personally and professionally:

> I've learnt a lot about myself in the year out and that's helping with my teaching.
>
> (SFD secondee 1988)

The expressions of having time to stand back and the chance to reflect came up in almost every interview I conducted. Secondees had experienced possibilities to see alternatives and review and re-frame their daily work and educational values. The chance to visit other schools, to communicate and co-operate with colleagues outside their own staff and with tutors, had not only modified their attitudes to teaching but opened more general insights into curriculum change, school management and development across the authority. These experiences have made many secondees more confident, even daring to question instructions of the management or dodge them.

Colleagues have noticed these changes and secondees have been told:

> I'm not the same person I was a year ago.
>
> (Aspinwall, 1989)

As regards the success of personal development, this quotation speaks for itself. It indicates an enthusiasm which is a catalyst, if not precondition, of successful innovation.

Another question is how far personal affections and changes of this sort, in this case certainly influenced by the quality of the tutors, can also be achieved by secondments exclusively to institutions of higher education. The combinations of school-focused secondment with formal assignments leading to the Diploma in Education or even the M.Ed., as in the first year of the Initiative (1986/87), was dropped by the authority as a compulsory element in the second and third year. University staff regretted this loss of postgraduates and expected a dilution of academic substance in the secondees' training and in schools (Rudduck and Wilcox, 1988). The problem is complicated and touches, as mentioned above, the very structure of school-based, school focused and academic staff development. For the authority, the central purpose of secondment is school reform, not personal promotion. Nevertheless, secondees still have the chance to use the SFD experience as a source for accreditation purposes.

Compared with the structure of in-service training in West Germany where universities are hardly involved, I appreciate the importance of the academic element for INSET and school reform in Britain. Some of the Sheffield M.Ed. theses I saw, successfully combined school focus and academic standards. This partnership of full-time university staff as well as tutors of the Sheffield Initiative can serve as a model for West German improvements.

I have treated the question of whole staff development in an earlier section and explained some barriers to it in the structure of school management and decision-making processes. The following paragraphs will analyze these problems in a wider context, starting from the seeming contradiction that, on the one hand, the vast majority of teachers saw the necessity and reasons for changes in schools: 'Changing attitudes of children to school; disenchantment of a growing minority of students who are "voting with their feet"; "changing needs of society", "technological and social change"; unemployment, falling rolls, the new GCSE examination, school mergers, etc; and, on the other hand, sometimes a lack of confidence that schools were able to follow the authority's initiative' (Fulker *et al.*, 1987). So secondees, in contrast to their personal development, were quite often disappointed about the small or slow changes in school ('still banging your head against the same barriers'; 2 December 1988), and on returning full-time to their schools felt inclined to deny or disguise what they had learned during secondment, because the system was not fully ready to utilize their offer (Rudduck and Wilcox, 1988).

Fulker *et al.*, 1987, largely confirm international findings (see Bolam *et al.*, above) about the conditions of successful staff development: whole staff commitment, open-mindedness and 'climate for change', regard to pace of effective change, to cross-curricular implications, flexible management, communication skills within staff, commitment of head and assistance from the LEA. Aspects of school climate favourable to innovation were neatly summed up by Aspinwall *et al.*, (1987): trust and respect between colleagues, readiness to face and work through difficulties and to share responsibility, straightforward communication, group work skills, regular staff meetings as a 'safe place to share experiences' and patience with small steps and conflicts. Commissions which built on previous projects and were planned in connection with or integrated with other innovations in school stood a better chance of success. Most of these aspects mark pre-conditions, before the beginning of innovations, as well as favourable factors needing to be achieved during its progress. Another momentum for success, of course, was the quality and qualification of secondees as innovators: their abilities to understand, sympathize, co-operate, organize and lead, and their credibility with staff. In some cases secondees were not chosen because of these qualities, but because no appropriate person volunteered or because of staffing or timetable problems. I shall return to this management perspective later.

The Sheffield Curriculum Initiative has affected all the secondary schools within the authority. But the scope and intensity of change are different in individual schools and in departments of the same school. In general, developments in the area of content/subject matter are more visible than in the areas of assessment, teaching method and teacher-student interaction. Several schools have implemented integrated programmes of work for the 11–13 age range, e.g. science, humanities, in order to better match their offerings to all school children and to facilitate mixed ability teaching. At the same time some have introduced modular courses, or, after closer contacts with feeder junior and middle schools, have reduced the number of teachers in the lower classes, extended the form tutor role and pastoral work and introduced more active and experiential learning. The LEA evaluation indicates that there is more attention to social development, more co-operative and group work, more practical and project work involving exploration of neighbourhood and communities and more flexibility in teaching style. Concerning increased responsibilities and self-decision of learners regarding their own learning processes, resistance against change has been more stubborn (for positive examples see Aspinwall, 1988c).

Another area of comparative resistance has been and still is that of school management, but headteachers not only report better relationships and co-operation between staff, but also an improved quality of discussion and more participation in staff meetings: evidently junior staff, in spite of the hierarchy, take a greater part in decision-making processes, are more ready to express their interests in staff meetings and try to practise a more collegial approach to management. At the same time senior management, at least in some schools, seems to be more careful to ensure staff commitment and participation. This has been accompanied by a 'lifting of morale' and motivation of teachers in a time of public criticism (SFD Tutorial Team, 1988a; Aspinwall, 1988a, 1987a).

To understand the comparatively slow progress in this area, one has to take into account that the Sheffield reform has fostered a 'new assertiveness' of teachers which calls for a new management style. (Rudduck and Wilcox, 1988; Fulker *et al.*, 1987) speak of a 'completely new element' in *all* Sheffield secondary schools, a 'new dimension' which can be quite 'threatening' to traditional management. The secondees' experience and teachers' desire to work as equals function, so to speak, as a horizontal force in a vertical, namely hierarchical structure. A headteacher has the fearful fantasy that secondees come back to his school 'as moles to overturn things' (Rudduck and Wilcox, 1988).

Apparently some headteachers feel a little isolated, and they, as well as their management team, need some support in finding new, more participative or democratic styles of leadership: the management training of heads, internationally, has a rather short history. The actual change in this direction, in Britain as well as in West Germany, up to now still seems to be hesitant, because it is bound up with more general changes in public legislation and administration. The development in Sheffield is encouraging. Personally, I saw a Sheffield school with very democratic decision-making procedures. Realizing that this development is closely connected with an increase of the 'ownership' of change by teachers, and recognizing the problems of some heads, the authority has established the Management Support Team sustained by seconded headteachers, SFD and CAR tutors and outside consultants.

Conclusion

A German colleague with more than a decade of experience in organization development and staff consultation, Wilfried Schley, has used observed structures of personal crises, including Bowlby's (1980) research on *Loss, Sadness and Depression* as a model for a concept of school reform. Accordingly to Schley, school developments do not move in straight lines but in spirals symptomatic of crises. And the stages they pass may be described as:

— leaving and loss of everyday routine;
— phase of denial (not to admit, ignore, skate over, suppress, seek refuge in activity);
— phase of rebellion (look for culprits, aggressions, reproaches, fury, helplessness, desperation, self-reproaches);

— phase of surrender (resignate, resign to one's fate, accept, develop indifference, function without share);
— phase of reorientation (see the world with different eyes, discover new values, take courage, find new ways);
— the way leads forward (Schley, 1988).

If I look back at my Sheffield experience, all this sounds much too negative. Admittedly, schools in West Germany and in Britain can be seen to be in a crisis. In West Germany they are in danger of losing the motivation and engagement of many of their best students: losing the substance of 'education'. In Britain the educational freedom and enthusiasm of teachers is threatened by a government introducing principles of business and 'wealthism' into a realm of different structure (Bassey, 1987, 1988). Wilfried Schley's analogy may explain some of the difficulties reformers are bound to meet. Any real or 'radical' change, of persons or institutions, brings about symptoms of Schley's crisis spiral. Different groups and persons, instead of being united as a whole staff in opinion and endeavour from the beginning, may find themselves at different phases of the crisis spiral. They can help each other to be more patient, flexible and tolerant of deviating positions. Outside consultants can also help them with this insight and with reaching the phase of 'reorientation'. I saw the tutors of the Sheffield School-Focused Development programme fulfil their share of this difficult task.

I was very much impressed with the way the tutor team as a whole demonstrated what partnership is and thus gave a model to secondees and the wider educational community, of equality and co-operation within staff, a model which the secondees as teachers could apply to their colleagues and pupils in school. The tutor team had weekly sessions in order to plan and evolve their working practices. In addition to the weekly planning meeting, the team spent some days working on their own development, updating and exchanging information and thinking through new initiatives.

Remembering points four to seven of Ray Bolam *et al.*, mentioned above, for future stages of the Sheffield reform, I would like to recommend a certain extension of the work of the Tutor Team in school: by including more observation of lessons and team teaching, more direct feedback at the chalk face and on-site coaching including consultation of whole staff on the organization development line. Such a change of emphasis towards the element of school-based work in the Initiative, may be realistic at a time when long-term secondment is on the retreat because of financial bottlenecks and political handicaps.

Fritz Bohnsack

The Sheffield Curriculum Initiative is a unique venture of innovation in Britain and without any parallel in West Germany. In the European and international perspective it is more than desirable, it is necessary that the Sheffield approach should be continued and further developed. The struggle of education to preserve its autonomy and find out better ways of teaching than in the past, against outside political principles and forces, is of exemplary, if not archetypal value and importance.

References

ALLERBECK, K. and HOAG, W. (1985) *Jugend ohne Zukunft?* München; Piper.

ANWYLL, S. (1988) *Primary SFS: Back in school*, Sheffield (mimeo).

ASPINWALL, K. (1986) *SFS: 'An idea has found its time' – Some initial responses to Sheffield's School-Focused Secondment programme*, Sheffield (mimeo).

ASPINWALL, K. (1987a) *Insider evaluator.* Paper given at the BERA annual conference, Manchester 1987 (Mimeo).

ASPINWALL, K. (1987b) *Interviews with secondees: Report no 1. The process of selection.* Sheffield (Mimeo).

ASPINWALL, K. (1987c) *Interviews with secondees: Report no 2: Attitudes and aspirations*, Sheffield (mimeo).

ASPINWALL, K. (1987d) *A climate for change: A report on the first year of Sheffield's School Focused Secondment initiative*, Sheffield (mimeo).

ASPINWALL, K. (1988a) *Curriculum change across schools.* BEMAS conference April 1988 (mimeo).

ASPINWALL, K. (1988b) *'Uncompleted business' : Interviews with secondees, Report no 3*, Sheffield (mimeo).

ASPINWALL, K. (1988c) *SFS/SFD. 'I learn best when...': Emerging changes in classroom experience*, Sheffield (mimeo).

ASPINWALL, K. (1988d) *Perceptions of SFS/D.* Sheffield (mimeo).

ASPINWALL, K. (1989) *'A bit of the sun': Teacher development through an LEA curriculum initiative manuscript.* Manuscript in P. Woods (ed); (1989) *Working for teacher development*, Peter Francis, Dereham, Norfolk.

ASPINWALL, K. and NIXON, J. (1986) *Managing change: A team approach.* A brief report of a two-day INSET programme for Sheffield LEA's SFD secondees held at Helbourne/Westbourne House Teachers Centres on 16th and 17th September 1986 (mimeo).

ASPINWALL, K. and NIXON, J. (1987) *Report on the conference 'The co-ordination of School Focused Secondment' for in-school co-ordinators* – Chesterfield, November 1987 (mimeo).

ASPINWALL, et al. (no date) *Curriculum development initiatives: Some factors influencing successful outcomes*, Sheffield (mimeo).

BASSEY, M. (1987) *A challenge to the ideology of the education reform bill;* Inaugural lecture 16 November 1987, School of Education, Trent Polytechnic.

BASSEY, M. (1988) 'Schools for conviviality'. *Education Now* May/June 1988, pp. 13–15.

BOHNSACK, F. (1987) 'Der Werte- und Verhaltenswandel in Gesellschaft und Jugend und seine Bedeutung für die Schule', *Die Deutsche Schule*, 79(4), pp. 421–429.

BOLAM, R. *et al.*, (1985) Effective inservice. In Hopkins, D. (Ed.) *Inservice Training and Educational Development: An International Survey*, London, Croom Helm, pp. 263–311.

BOWLBY, J. (1980) *Loss, Sadness and Depression*, London, The Hogarth Press.

BRANDES, D. and GINNIS, P. (1986) *A Guide to Student-Centred Learning*, Oxford, Basil Blackwell.

CITY OF SHEFFIELD EDUCATION COMMITTEE (1988) *Curriculum Policy*, Sheffield (mimeo).

ERMERT, K. (Ed.) (1987) *'Gute Schule' – Was ist das?* Loccumer Protokolle 17/1986, Rehburg-Loccum, Evangelische Akademie Loccum.

FISCHER, A. *et al.*, (Eds) (1982) *Jugend '81: Lebensentwürfe, Alltagskulturen, Zukunftsbilder*, Vol 1, Opladen, Leske.

FULKER, P., REGAN, P., and THOMPSON, J. (1987) *The Sheffield SFS programme. An evaluation: Management implications for schools and LEA*, Sheffield (mimeo).

FULLAN, M. (1985) 'Change processes and strategies at the local level', *The Elementary School Journal*, 85(3), pp. 391–421.

GREIG, S., PIKE, G. and SELBY, D. (1987) *Earthrights: Education As If the Planet Mattered*, London, WWF and Kogan Page.

HAENISCH, H. (1986) 'Gute und schlechte Schulen im Spiegel der empirischen Schulforschung', *Westermanns Pädagogische Beiträge*, 37(7/8), pp. 19–23.

HARGREAVES, A. (1982) 'The rhetoric of school-centred innovation, *Journal of Curriculum Studies*, 14(3), pp. 251–266.

HOPKINS, D. (Ed.) (1985) *Inservice Training and Educational Development: An International Survey*, London, Croom Helm.

HURRELMANN, K., ROSEWITZ, B. and WOLF, H.K. (1985) *Lebensphase Jugend: Eine Einführung in die sozialwissenschaftliche Jugendforschung*, Weinheim, Juventz.

KLAFKI, W. (1985) 'Konturen eines neuen Allgemeinbildungskonzepts, in W. Klafki *Neue Studien zur Bildungstheorie und Didaktik*, Weinheim, Beltz, pp. 12–30.

KLAGES, H. (1985) *Wertorientierungen im Wandel*, Frankfurt, Campus.

KLEBER, E.W. (1985) 'Ökologische Pädagogik oder Umwelterzierhung?' In Twellmann, W. (Ed.) *Handbuch Schule und Unterricht*, Vol 7.2, Düsseldorf, Schwann, pp. 1194–1210.

NIXON, J. (Ed.) (1987) *Curriculum Change : The Sheffield Experience*. USDE Papers in education. Sheffield: Division of Education/University of Sheffield.

PIKE, G. and SELBY, D. (1988) *Global Teacher, Global Learner*, London, Hodder and Stoughton.

RUDDUCK, J. (1988) *Partnership in in-service: The Sheffield initiative*: A paper for the UCET conference, November 1988 (mimeo).

RUDDUCK, J. and WILCOX, B. (1988) 'Issues of ownership and partnership on school-centred innovation: the Sheffield experience', *Research Papers in Education*, 3(3), pp. 157–179.

SCHLEY, W. (1988) 'Organisationsentwicklung an Schulen, *Report Psychologie*, August 1988, pp. 11–20.

SFD TUTORIAL TEAM (1988a) *How to get the best out of SFD*, Sheffield (mimeo).

SFD TUTORIAL TEAM (1988b) *Introduction to Sheffield's School-Focused Development programme*, Sheffield (mimeo).

STEFFENS, U. (1986) 'Erkundungen zur Wirksamkeit und Qualität von Schule', *Die Deutsche Schule* 78(3), pp. 294–305.

STEFFENS, U. and BARGEL, T. (Eds) (1987/88) *Beiträge aus dem Arbeitskreis 'Qualität von Schule'*, Vol 1–4, Wiesbaden, Hessisches Institut für Bildungsplanung und Schulentwicklung.

8
Questioning the Franchise: A Personal View from Higher Education

Peter Clough

> People know what they do; they frequently know why they do what they do; but what they don't know is what what they do does...
>
> (Foucault, 1982)

What do we – in university and polytechnic departments of education – know of what we do to schools? And what effects do they have on us? I see schools as related to higher education (and in particular, the University) as in some respects like the way a bottling-plant in Barnsley, say, relates to the Coca-Cola Company of America. A powerful franchise invisibly binds the different communities as they live out their separate cultures.

By evoking structures of the franchise, I want to describe some of the impact which I think Sheffield LEA's SCI programme has had on the life of 'my own' institution; and to imagine some of the impressions which the Division of Education has left on the LEA. I suspect that there are some scars on both bodies.

I worked within an arm of the SCI[1] for two years and was very affected by it, personally and professionally. So what follows is – importantly – a personal view; it must be, not least because there is in the end no single, orthodox university or polytechnic 'view' or experience, just as no comprehensive LEA account could be drawn up. Maybe this is the first, if naive point to make: that the relationship between the LEA and the University was carried out in behaviours which were initially organized through formal institutional and symbolic structures – the Chief Education Officer negotiated with our Head of Department, for example – but the relationship was actual through the personal experiences of hundreds of people. Some of these experiences were positive, stimulating, productive, and gave rise in those instances to a feeling that the structured partnership was a good thing; some were pinched, frustrating and abortive, and made people blame 'the University' for being such-and-such, or 'the LEA' for being so-and-so. In the reality as I now see it, University and LEA structur-es – often blamed for arrests of relationships – became enabling or obstructive only in the hands of the individuals who called upon them.

In fact, I remember there was a deal of accommodation. A really good example of this was in the area of assignments and assessments. Recall that secondees on the programme could, if they wished, submit written accounts of their work for credit towards the award of a Diploma or M.Ed. within our Advanced Studies Programme (See, Preface). There were early problems: what *counted* as acceptable *work*? *Who* said it counted? How *written* did it have to be? For consider that, at that time, the Division was only just freeing itself from the grip of a very traditional credentialism deriving from the ownership of knowl-edge which the University at large demonstrates; consider that a fair number of secondees were carrying out 'practical' school-focused work which was vital in the doing but which would translate uneasily – and often pointlessly – into an essay form. In the event, a formula was worked out which not only went some way towards meeting the needs of all parties, but which in the process contributed to a much broader and more general springclean of many of the Division's forms and processes of assessment. (This is discussed in more detail below.) In the process, however, I recall many characterizations of a synthesized 'The University' (intransigent, 19th Century, out-of-touch, 'theoretical' (!)), and just as many of a notional 'The LEA'. Some of these characteriz-ations, crude though they are, nevertheless reflect real identities – or, at least, identities made more or less real through the experience of the 'structured partnership'.

A Matter of Principle

As a scheme for the first part of this chapter, I want to consider how the identity of the University met with that of the SCI as it is expressed through its foundation principles (see, Chapter 2). Three such principles are said to lie at the heart of SCI; if these principles are characteristic of SCI – if, indeed, they are its hallmark – it is worth asking what role the University had to play in their realization. This is also to ask whether these principles are characteristic of the University. These questions provide a frame for the discussion.

Learning to Change

SCI has attached a particular conception of learning. Learning, it is said, is much more of an *event* than we commonly suppose; if it has knowable structures, they may be better described by art than by psychology as it is commonly understood. Learning – the argument goes – must be made a problematic, its processes brought out from behind the crude correspondences of teaching intentions and examination schemes.

Through various activities within its programme, SCI has attempted to break open common conceptions and practices of learning. It started to do this, I feel, in time with the trepidation of interest in learning which projects like the TVEI Pilot prompted. Such realization of the immanence of learning in education has developed only recently; generally, it has not been fashionable to think about learning. It has been taken for granted by educators as an invisible means of a manifest competence. Rather, we have generally put much more effort into deciding what and how things shall be taught then wondering how it is that anything is ever learned. Maybe it is too much of a mystery; or maybe learning has simply been surrendered by teachers to the psychologists who occupied its ground so possessively in the 1960s and early '70s. (There are, of course, notable exceptions to this in work on the sociology of knowledge as well as in subject-specific developments, for example in English Studies).

In any event, learning as such has not been a central interest of teachers. Nor has it much interested INSET-providers in the University, who – in common, it must be said, with colleagues throughout the UK – have offered a range of courses which in the selection of content and the style of their delivery have been little concerned with the situation of learning. Up until the last few years, the pre- and in-service courses in my own department have been conservative in their conception, in their event and no doubt in their effects. Further, any teaching *about* learning has often been as narrow as the channels *of* learning which have been open to students. Frequently such interest in learning as there is, is directed onto the phenomena of *other people's learning*, and does not itself feed reflexively into educationists' own practice as learners and teachers and researchers. Within this practice the conceptions of learning and of knowledge which many educationists carry around with them, and which inform our teaching, appear grimly narrow, chauvinistic and under licence to outdated psychological models.

This is partly explained – though clearly not justified – by the association of University Departments of Education INSET with Higher Degree programmes, and with the constipations that go with accreditation structures. The arrival in my department of some one hundred secondees in September 1986 immediately pointed up the stress on this link. Using the now defunct 'pooling' system, the LEA had freed an unprecedented number of teachers – but on condition of their following award-bearing courses. Hence their commissions had, at least formally, to be mediated through Higher Education; more specifically, the characteristic task of re-definition of learning had to be shared in institutions whose models of learning and knowledge were most typically expressed in well-sedimented forms of assignment and assessment.

When the first cohort of Curriculum Development Initiative secondees arrived at the University, it rapidly became clear that this habit of practice and attitude was not up to meeting their needs. At the outset of the programme neither we nor the secondees had much positive idea of quite what was called for in the way of a 'new' INSET, and University-led sessions often followed an implicit view that exposure to (other people's well-referenced) ideas would somehow infect what teachers took back to school. The secondees came, however, with commissions practically related to their schools, sets of tasks situated in urgent needs for change; they were charged with bringing about change as a condition of secondment, and as a condition of credibility back in school. The needs they expressed were concrete, calling for concrete support. Although we learned to give some of this, I was one of those who made little initial accommodation, seeing the new secondees as no different in their needs from the students I had become used to working with. I wanted to refer their concrete problems to schemes of issues and ideas which were at the centre of *my* work, and *my* way of working. At the heart of the teaching enterprise was an uncritical assumption about what should be learned; this tacit justification was at best only obliquely related to the real needs of the secondees. Those needs called rather for a logic of discovery.

For my part, I feel it took quite a long time to trust myself and the secondees sufficiently for me to let go the instinct to control learning. This experience goes near the heart of the problem of UDE-based INSET. For, of course, this instinct was shored up by the expectations of many of the secondees, who quite reasonably expected to be informed by the University. That expectation is a function of the control over knowledge which the University exerts structurally, and which is made real in the expectations of it. Every last one of its structures is a powerful licence on what shall count as knowledge; all other institutional forms of education are effectively franchises on this model. This is – one might say – simply a fact, but it raises important questions about any claims we might make about real partnership in learning when our own structures so powerfully pre-determine the epistemology which is at the centre of the activity.

This problem – which could be called one of power epistemology – is similarly deep in the ground of the next principle.

Equality of Opportunity

The second key principle of SCI cited is that of equality of opportunity, taken to include situations of social class and disability as well as race and gender. It finds its more general and most apparent aspect within SCI in consideration of a substantial majority of under-achieving and minimally-qualified young people leaving school at the earliest opportunity; their experience of schooling may be variably explained in terms of this intervolved platform of issues. SCI further attempts self-consciousness by recognizing the inequalities inherent in its own structures[2].

Again, the equal opportunities question is actually an epistemological one; it is only contingently about the specific interests of black, say, or female or working-class students; it is rather, essentially, about the issue of who determines what shall count as knowledge. This issue itself is of course expressed through the situation of subordinated populations, but questions about the process of that subordination can be regressed into the fundamental question of *Who says what counts?*

In the University, the issue of equal opportunities takes on an aspect of the absurd. The University is a vigorously white, masculine and elitist institution, and its relationship with its students is indispensably patrician. As guardians of what counts as knowledge, University staff habitually arbitrate between the known and the would-be knower – frequently, of course, standing in his or her way or, rather, strewing phylacteries like so many obstacles. This is true of the University at large, though perhaps in the softer parts (of its Arts faculty, maybe?) the idea of a more negotiable knowledge is worked through its pedagogy. But structurally – through Ordinace, Statute and Regulation – structurally, the University cannot avoid measuring the stuff of knowledge through entrance and exit criteria which have little regard for the social purposes of that knowledge, and even less for the way in which people experience it.

It is difficult to say whether and how staff in Education Departments are different from staff in other departments. We should remember, however, that staff appointments are made to the University; its appointing committees are bound to value academic performance and research potential. Most staff appointed to UDEs – and in particular to my own – already have at least one Higher Degree (though not always in education). A few have distinguished research profiles. Their ever-receding school teaching experience – as distinct from their remedial doses of 'recent and relevant' practice – in all probability reached its peak as a member of senior staff (in many cases in Grammar schools). Staff in UDEs are by definition successful graduates of an academic tradition which in the context of the University it is difficult to resist.

Of course, the University has a broad equal opportunities policy, and the Division of Education has a slightly more elaborated form of this. But its performance generally in the area of equal opportunities must be tied – and evaluated – structurally with the models of knowledge and learning discussed above. To be sure we have worked to make our courses more accessible, but we have hardly begun to erode – either within the department or in schools – the inequalities which are a condition of our own status.

This 'we' is an identity which comes of a particular history of practice, and all the habits of attitude and conditions of work and service which characterize that practice. A University Department of Education is by nature alienated from schools; although it is concerned *with* school issues, the rhythm of its daily concerns and the meanings of its issues are not those *of* the school. These differences are palpable and were, I know, felt in similar measure by temporary staff and seconded teachers. Many secondees – and a considerable number of temporary staff – came to the University with the same disabling sense of their marginality which children feel in school. These feelings are effective evaluations of our equal opportunities policies and practices.

Organization for Change

The third principle of SCI recognizes that the way all people relate to one another within an organization profoundly affects that organization's capacity for change. Thus development of organizational structures, curriculum and staff are indispensably related; any such developments colour the whole culture of the school. This sort of view has led most visibly to a particular conception and organization of INSET which is distinct from the traditional model.

When Sheffield University was asked to participate in the development of the LEA's SFS programme, it was ill-equipped to do so. It was no more unready than any other department might have been in a similar situation, I think, but nevertheless – by virtue of its traditions of structure and practice – it lacked a framework of resource which would be up to meeting the sort of demands which were shortly to be made of it.

Firstly, we were curiously placed to take on a programme concerned with whole-institution change, because as a department we ourselves enjoy few common purposes. We are at most a collection of broadly sympathetic individuals. That individuality goes back to the contract of our employment, and to the 'jealously guarded' right of academic autonomy. We are united by little apart from this contract. As a department, we attach no political view (though we are formally committed to 'comprehensive principles'), nor have we any other determining 'colour' of social or educational theory. We can have very little in the way of policy (the more so as market forces determine where and how we should situate our work). Individual tutors work fairly exclusively with separate populations of pre- or in-service students who have between them few structures for dialogue (or means of organizing a political voice). We develop practices through committee structures, and have few mechanisms for staff development, course development or quality control. Of course there is collaboration, but our federated activities do not add up to any sense of a collective.

Secondly, the focus of our work with students is normally individualized. HE institutions typically recruit individuals primarily; occasionally, pairs or even trios may come from a school, but this is rare. These individuals come with agendas which, although they may relate to their professional context, have been personally–identified. It is at least tacitly recognized that the working through of these concerns is for the profit of the individual. By contrast, SCI brought to the institutions groups of teachers (five per school in the first year) charged with school-focused commissions which would realize change primarily in school.

Following on from this point, there is thirdly the question of where (and therefore in many ways how) these issues should be worked. One of the characteristic features of the SCI project is the site of its processes – they largely happen in schools. In the HE institutions, however, teachers come away from the site of their practice in order to study and research. However much tutorial support focuses on the expressed needs of the individual teacher, it remains largely ignorant of the context of his or her situation; it cannot engage with the empirical forces of issue and interest which actually prompt a real research problem. Thus individuals are removed from the site of that shared experience and discourse which is the seat of their professional knowledge and identity.

Finally, our staffing situation was deficient, firstly in numbers but equally in terms of interests and ways of working. Most importantly, few members of my own department have any training whatever in designing and delivering INSET – and particularly not in schools – and most had no experience before taking up the post. Nor do we have any systematic professional development to meet the need. Most – as I did – make it up as they go along, and most have become adept and successful within the received tradition of accreditable INSET.

It was quite clear that we would never be able to staff courses (whatever they were going to look like) with available staff from the departmental establishment. The department was short-staffed in any event, and then there were clearly areas of specialism – and generalism – which we could not presume to address. So additional, short-term contract staff were subsequently recruited to fill full- and part-time positions. These eight temporary lecturers were mostly seconded to us, variously from LEA schools and advisory, from research projects, a national commission and another university. In common, they had all worked as teachers, most occupied (or had until recently occupied) relatively senior positions in school and all were positive applicants for the new venture. Perhaps most importantly they were all already occupied in their work with the issues which lay at the heart of the SCI (and for which purposes they were, after all, recruited): the redefinition of learning; the equality of opportunity; the development of assessment forms ... and so on.

It is no exaggeration to say that the staff brought in in this way were charged with working through a programme which was – point by point – more vital to schools than anything else on the departmental prospectus. It is really to them that the University owes the relative successes of the structured partnership. But few of those staff recruited to deliver the University's programme found it a satisfying experience; they were frustrated by a structure and culture which they did not find inclusive, and which engaged awkwardly with that of the schools they were working in. Their experience reflects the way in which the SCI was never really integrated within the whole culture of the department's work. Although some seven of the tenured staff worked part-time in various arms of the programme (with its one hundred students) in the first year, there was always a paradoxical sense of its marginality within an 'orthodox' work of the Division.

And, of course, in entrusting a deal of the work to temporary staff, we failed to take proper advantage of the opportunities for our own development which the programme offered us. For it is very clear that our own organization for change needs a deal of attention.

In the present section I have rehearsed the central principles of the SCI as I see them impinging on some of the structures of my department[3]. In the next section I shall look in more detail at some aspects of departmental practice in the light of SCI.

Re-Defining 'The Practical'

A need to re-define the idea of the practical has emerged from some of the distinctions made between 'the University' and 'the LEA' agendas and 'ways of working'. The traditional ways of working sometimes rubbed up against each other and were sometimes contradictory. We were made uncomfortable so many times by wanting teachers to introduce into their reported work insights from the literature, say, which they saw as irrelevant. Their reasonable claim was made that work carried out on secondment should primarily serve the commissions and needs of the seconding schools; to be sure, many had used the literature as integral parts of their commissions, but elegantly-referenced assessment for the purposes of accreditation was of minor importance. In the early days, some secondees argued that work – for example, the revision of a second-year science course – was completed to the extent that it affected practice in schools; what, they asked, was the justification for writing a critical account of it?

As a scheme for this second section, I propose to take some closely-related areas of the Division's work – assignments, assessment and teacher-research – and discuss the qualities of these developments of 'the practical' in the light of the SCI experience.

Peter Clough

Who Says What Counts?

The greater part of what is carried on in the name of INSET in the Division is tied to higher degree structures, and has until relatively recently been conservative of a traditional epistemology. Consequently, the pattern of this work typically featured:

— a selection of materials determined by the tutor according to criteria largely invisible to the student;
— a programme of teaching events designed to 'release' those materials serially, at intervals controlled by the tutor;
— a style of release which kept the locus of control with the tutor;
— a form of assignment which largely reflected a literally–rather than empirically–situated exercise;
— a form of assessment designed to reproduce the traditional ownership of knowledge.

Considerable erosion of this pattern has taken place over the last years and, for my part at least, the experience of SCI accelerated the process. It was clear from the beginning that these sedimented forms would not meet the needs of the programme, and a more sensitive scheme was worked out with LEA staff. For all that, within CDI we soon ran up against problems which appeared to polarize LEA and University views. From the schools' point of view, the University appeared unwilling to bend its assessment practices sufficiently to meet their needs. Underlying this was a view about the value of 'writing up'. The schools appeared to feel that secondees should not be using their valuable time turning out products for assessment which do not contribute significantly to the work they are trying to do in schools. They felt that if secondees had participated in change processes and had made a substantial contribution to those processes, then that should be enough. Such participation requires thought – they argued – and is not just about 'experience'. People think about their experiences and use those thoughts to guide action, and to generate further experiences which they reflect on ... and so on. Writing up may be interesting, but it is in the end a luxury.

On the other hand, the University staff within CDI felt that given the aims of the SCI programmes – which are to do with profound changes in the way that teachers think about themselves and their roles – the self-interrogation and critical reflection required by the writing-up process are indispensable. We saw the schools as not giving secondees enough personal space for critical thought and self-development. Teachers are – we wrote – members of a literary culture in which most educated people have certain competencies. To assume that secondees do not need to utilize these competencies to examine their experiences is to underestimate the benefit they would derive from the actual writing-up process. We felt that the accusing view of the University as only requiring a product because of traditional assessment practices was a red herring.

This often heated argument was finally resolved by a process of negotiation between the partners which, far from damaging any institutional principle, actually went some way towards developing and refining their characteristic practices. It is worth rehearsing here the justification that was finally arrived at, as an example of careful accommodation which profited both partners.

The argument we developed saw assessment as an important part of the SCI programme, not primarily for the part it played in determining whether individuals passed the Diploma (though this is undoubtedly important) but because it is an aspect of the processes of *evaluation* which must lie at the heart of the whole SCI venture. In a sense – we argued – SCI itself could be seen as a sophisticated complex of evaluation and assessment processes related to the fundamental aims of innovation and change. Within these aims, the institution-based forms of the SCI programme could provide a particular structure for their realization; we should find forms of assessment which could communicate some of the vigour of the processes involved and the value of their outcomes.

Together we argued – and agreed – that change takes place within given *communities* and within given *traditions*. SCI is a network of communities which derives its coherence as a programme from a set of communal interests; change within these communities must be understood and signalled between the communities, and finally validated by them. Of course, it must be accepted that those communities are themselves expressions of particular traditions of practice and theory, of policy and legislation and so on. So an account of change within a community must take some stock of its place within that larger evolving tradition – as it is reported in the literature, as well as experienced in visits outside of Sheffield; otherwise, how could it be recognized *as a change*?

In summary, it was argued that innovation is understood when it is critically described within the traditions of a particular community, in an account which relates what 'I' am doing and thinking to what others are doing and thinking. In these respects, assessment forms within the University part of the SCI should be about formalizing the processes of evaluation given with any innovation. This is to insist that there is a rational and desirable case for the careful communication of the processes and products of SCI innovations *even before* any involvement of the institutions.

The basic criterion for the evaluation of SCI innovations (and therefore the assignments which report them) was derived from the above arguments; it is the *communicability* of lessons learned from the experience of change. The characteristic question which might be used to evaluate an assignment is thus:

> Is the value of the work as reported sufficiently understood (by those who are reporting it) so that its structures can be located in the traditions of practice, and its meanings expressed in a form accessible – and enabling – to others?

This sounds a bit contrived, and not a little fudged, and I now suspect that the account did more to satisfy the University than excite the teachers. But I should emphasize that at the time this was a 'real' position worked out within CDI by LEA and school staff as well as the University, and one which was at least formally acceptable to all as a criterion for the design and assessment of assignments.

Of course, it is clear that any usefulness of this form of argument depends ultimately on a set of assignment forms up to delivering its particular view of the nature of change. These were developed between LEA and University Staff and range through such forms as the personal journal, for example, the group planning document, the small-scale research project, the critical presentation of curriculum materials and so on. In each case, rough protocols were established for guidance, and the need for critical perspective was emphasized as a condition of com-municability. Generally speaking the work produced in this way has not met separated school and University demands as such, but has rather re-defined the common ground of their interests.

Modifications to other (non-SCI) areas of the Division's work have kept pace with, if not actually followed these developments. The greater part of assignment work undertaken within our Advanced Studies Programme (leading to Diploma/M.Ed.) is empirically-situated and mostly school-focused. As far as formal procedures are concerned, we have abolished examinations and all marks other than pass/fail; we have done away with the Distinction in the M.Ed.; discipline-based teaching has practically vanished; 'Independent Studies' – which attempt to meet individual needs not catered for within our modular ASP – have been established; assignments may be submitted by groups for joint credit; we have established that non-literal media may be acceptable for assessment. And we are currently working on a form of dissertation-study which will not see its product merely gathering dust on a library shelf.

These developments reflect changes in the content and style of courses: Effective Schooling, Collaborative Group Work, Innovation and Change, School-based INSET, Assessment, and Curricular Approaches to Learning Difficulties are only a few of the many modules which, in the negotiation of their content and the manner of their delivery, are sincere attempts to organize practice-based study around the needs of teachers and schools.

Whose Data is it Anyway?

Now a major instrument of these developments – within the ASP and the SCI – has been teacher-research method, most commonly carried out by individual teachers. It is at this point that I would like to re-introduce some of the points made in my first section about determination and ownership of knowledge, and equality of opportunity: '*Who* says *what* counts?' is still the question.

Teacher research provides a way of working with teachers which in representing the culture of school as so many data brings a new discipline to bear on the experience of professional practice. Thus teacher research is a part of the necessary compromise with schools which HE institutions have made within Higher Degree programmes; for while the data may be those situated by the individual teacher, the discipline – in whatever variation of the form it is realized – derives from structures accountable elsewhere: in research methodology, examination procedures and so on. In this respect, it is a good move towards partnership worthy of the name. But it is not unproblematic.

If you examine the moment of that relationship further, there is also a sense in which it may be a *legerdemain* which says 'Look, we have given you executive power', while implicitly retaining the power of approval. For as long as teacher research is tied to Higher Degree structures, the direction of its processes and the validation of its outcomes rests with HE institutions rather than with the situation of the research. The 'Action Research Cycle' (see, for example, Bell, 1985) is a good illustration of an 'alternative' INSET structure which actually subordinates the professional knowledge and experience of the teacher to an academically-controlled schema. It is a trick. It attaches the plausible ideology of the democratization of educational research, but it manages to be both teacherist and chauvinistic: it appears to place the teacher at the centre of the research process, but by its selective legitimation of method it makes sure that validation remains in the hands of the academics. For above all, the action research cycle makes the situation of a research susceptible to an assessment framework outside of its own reality; its processes and outcomes become accountable within an itinerary indifferent to the political experiences of particular situations. It actually hardly matters what the topic and purposes are. Indeed, the universal applicability of the cycle surely damages its claim to '(stand) in opposition to a dominant tradition of positivistic social science' (Bell, 1987). But Bell does not seem alarmed by his claim that 'what was once a radical movement seems now to be developing into the new orthodoxy' (1985, p. 175).

Nor is he, apparently, aware of whose orthodoxy it is. The collective outcomes of teacher research feed a discourse which is developing in HE institutions, for it is HE staff who write *about* teacher research, not schools and teachers (other than as part of Higher Degree work). It gives a new and apparently moral engagement to our work. But we should wonder about its possibility as a radically new, democratic paradigm of HE-LEA collaboration. If it is good, teacher research can help individual teachers articulate the underlying causes of dissatisfaction in a persuasive, substantiated manner, and so enhance professional and school development. At its best, it might draw attention to social justice. But at its worst it may be a liberal sham which does more to meet the needs of academics than the political interests of teachers, schools and society. So we must be uncomfortable about teacher research, particularly where it is carried out by individuals – powerful or not within their school contexts – and particularly when it is to be assessed for Higher Degree accreditation.

Conclusion: Time to Think

In *Issues of ownership and partnership in school-centred innovation: the Sheffield Experience*, Rudduck and Wilcox (1988) explore some aspects of the SCI as they experienced it (in their roles as Professor of Education and Chief Adviser respectively). In the concluding paragraphs, they describe the 'interesting tension' exposed by HE staff performing a 'support role in addition to the tutorial one'. The presence of HE in the partnership should – by contrast, they imply – 'symbolise a continuing commitment to reflection, research and critique'; so,

> ...if HE tutors perform largely as 'quasi-advisers', this could lead to a major loss of perspective and ultimately of quality. What teachers desperately need is time to come to terms with and understand what they are doing. Such understanding cannot be won without all the partners in the partnership recognising that 'real change requires intellectual effort' (Kanter, 1983, p. 23)   Rudduck and Wilcox, 1988, p. 178.

I feel that this goes innocently to the heart of the franchise which relates HE to schools; it is difficult to avoid the assumption of HE's role as maker of terms (to 'come to') and as guarantor of quality – a quality defined by 'intellectual effort' (whatever that is). It is a bleak image which sees us (in HE) always just over the finishing line urging a better effort – 'an intellectual effort' – from a runner disabled not by shortage of time – nor even of intellect – but by our view of his or her effort as deficient in what it is that makes *us* different. Our understanding of schools is conditioned by the structures of that difference.

In this context, teachers' need for time is a red herring (unless we are going to apply through our research a political cunning which will persuade policy-makers that they do). What they really need is support from someone who will not tell them that they need time – they know that and they can't have it. Time – a particular sort of time – is something *we* have in distinction from schools. I understand that it is one of the characteristic tasks of my job to take time continually to re-work an understanding of particular issues as they are realized in a broad range of situations – in my case, in the field of Special Educational Needs. This is clearly distinct from the experience and brief of teachers and schools, though that very understanding depends on them not only for its data but ultimately for its value; the one cannot be understood without the other. But I have argued earlier that the culture of schools has in so many ways had to bow – however reluctantly – to the authority of the University that the dignities of their ways of knowing are distorted. To be sure teachers need time, but no more than *we* (in HE) need to make 'time to come to terms with and understand' what *we* are doing; to understand the distortions and to know more than anything – in Foucault's phrase – 'what what (we) do does.'

In trying out ideas for breaking the franchise, I am aware that there is a contradictory piety in my account: I am, after all, firmly on this side of the fence. But I believe that we need to do something about our relationship with schools, and soon – even before the implications of the Education Reform Act are felt. We should certainly think hard about INSET; for schools can only start to be partners worthy of the name if they can relate to HE with the power of their collective, its culture and its budget. They cannot be equals as long as individual teachers are recruited to teacher research programmes, and are contingents in a dialogue largely defined by the University (and if they are not really partners, then we are working with the illusion of partnership).

Less commodiously, we could do something about really redefining our Higher Degree structures, for the very terms of HD programmes – the terms of 'power epistemologies' – oppose the process of school-focused, culture-based INSET; deep in the heart of the HD programme is a view of learning and knowledge which can only issue as a set of legitimations.

More wildly, perhaps teacher education should be moved out of HE where a research ethic – even in the breach – mediates teachers and schools to us as so many data; in trying to understand the foreign culture of schools, it is impossible not to be infected with a research attitude. Or, less radically, at an individual level we might totally separate teacher educator and research functions so that we cannot attempt to do both; so that we can choose *either* to work with teachers *or* to try to understand them.

We certainly need, with LEAs and schools, to examine urgently our ways of working in mutual interest. But the hope for a 'powerful educational coalition that recognises the distinctive contribution of each of the (LEA and HE) partners' (Rudduck and Wilcox, *op. cit.*) is naive unless it takes for granted that the University's contribution has been distinctive in its powerful arbitration of what shall count as knowledge. Following the Education Reform Act, the creation of a market relation between Universities and schools may yet lead to a re-working of the power epistemology. Perhaps in the end it is this market which will break the hold which UDEs have; for schools, with their new budgetary powers, will have a much more powerful say in the valuation of knowledge as it is created in practice. Paradoxically, if handled properly by UDEs that very market-relation could do a deal to counter the evils of Thatcherism. Of course, schools – and policy-makers – will need educating to see and use UDEs in this new way and that will require UDEs indeed to develop a new cunning. This chapter, as a signal of a willingness to criticize ourselves, may also indicate what we can yet do in partnership with others.

Acknowledgments

The editors of this book gave me some valuable comment on the substance of this paper, as did Peter Hannon, David Jackson, Tim Kendall and Jon Nixon. The inaccuracies and the prejudices are – as they say – of course all mine.

Notes

1   When Sheffield LEA used the pooling system (in its last year) to second some 230 teachers, it was obliged to register them for award-bearing courses; they went in fairly equal numbers to the University's Division of Education and to Sheffied City Polytechnic's Education Department. Part of the University's cohort was made up of teachers from schools additionally-funded through the Lower Attaining Pupils Programme (LAPP), which developed its identity in Sheffield as the Curriculum Development Initiative (CDI). This programme was administered separately from, though was broadly similar in its aims and processes to that of the School-Focused Secondment programme at the University. Within the CDI, two of us from the University's permanent staff worked with three LEA-based Tutors: an Educational Psychologist, and two deputy headteachers seconded full-time from their posts. We worked with the management teams of the four project schools to identify and mount a core programme of study for the total of twenty teachers who would be seconded each term.

In the first year, this programme was organized centrally around topics which the participating schools' management teams had helped identify; in the first year these were 'Curriculum Learning and Assessment', 'Equal Opportunities', and 'Community Education'. All secondees followed a 'taster' programme within this core and further specialized within an aspect of these topics, relative to the particular school commission. It was projected that a third strand of study would be made up of individuals' 'own' particular interests, (though largely for reasons of time this scheme was never properly realised). The week was organized so that secondees could spend one day on the core programme, one day on each of the specialisms and personal interests, and the other two days in school.

Despite the fact that we University staff could devote a maximum of three-fifths of our week to the programme – I, for example, maintained as best I could a 'normal' Divisional load of teaching, research and administrative activities outside the SCI – it was agreed within the tutorial team that the five of us should all share all tasks. These included personal tutorship and – most importantly – a role as School Tutor, liaising with Headteacher, Senior Management Team and non-seconded staff.

Thus a fairly typical week for me would be spent on the first day in contribution to the core programme, on the second with a group – for example in the first term, a group of eight looking at Alternative Teaching and Learning Strategies – and on the third with the group of secondees from 'my' school, working on whole-school-related issues. Unlike the LEA-based staff, I had little extra time for vital school visits.

The programme changed in the second year, losing its 'core' and focusing more directly on the school commissions, though often through cross-school groups. Both I and the other University tutor left the programme after two years, and for its third and final year were replaced by a temporary lecturer working full-time on CDI with assistance from other tenured staff.

Although I worked principally within the CDI programme, I was also associated in a number of ways with the students, staff and processes of the larger SFS programme, and continue this involvement in an *ad hoc* way – for example contributing to the design of the SFD Special Needs core element. This paper is based on my broad experiences within the University, CDI, SFS/D and school programmes over the last three years.

2   The complex site of SCI – inside and outside of the schools – is of course a ground irradiated with inequalities licensed – and sometimes exploited – by status. Perhaps it is not surprising that such a controversial programme working up, down and across so many institutions should excite strong emotions, and evoke the will to power. At all levels of the partnership – in schools, HE and the central LEA – expressions of support and opposition alike have often prompted behaviours which ironically point up the centrality of the issue of equality of opportunity. Perhaps in all such projects there is bound to be a lot of destructive *ego* about (particularly where this has the fillip of a fat budget).

3   This chapter appears in a collection broadly descriptive rather than critical of the SCI; within that scheme I have begun an analysis of some of the structures of only one of the partners. I have dwelt, perhaps unequally, on reservations about the Division of Education's role in the SCI, and I have mentioned few of the many positive aspects of our place in the partnership. But if I have leant rather hard on the University, I have no rosy illusions about the structures and culture of the other partners. The same sort of job could have been done equally for the Polytechnic, for the LEA, its advisory, its individual schools and its SFD team. Such an analysis would reveal aspects of structure with strengths and weaknesses like those of the University – for, to be sure, trial of SCI's determining principles in each of these agencies would raise just as many doubts about *their* adequacy to deal with such an agenda. In this respect, it should be remembered that the effects of SCI are still emerging and continually being evaluated, and its celebration in these chapters will undoubtedly be qualified.

References

BELL, G. (1985) 'Can schools develop knowledge of their practice?' *School Organisation*, 2, pp. 175–184.

BELL, G. (1987) *Action research in the educational field: European Contexts*, paper presented to International Seminar, Department of Education, University Cattolica Del Sacro Cuore, Milan, Italy, 21–23 May.

FOUCAULT, M. (1982) 'Personal communication to the authors', in DREYFUS, H. and RABINOV, P. (1982) *Michael Foucault: Beyond Structuralism and Hermeneutics*, Brighton, Harvester Press.

RUDDUCK, J. and WILCOX, B. (1988) 'Issues of ownership and partnership in school-centred innovation: the Sheffield experience', *Research Papers in Education*, Vol. 3, 3 pp. 157–179.

9

Implications for LEAs: The End of an Era or the Forerunner of a New?

Tim Brighouse

Sheffield's curriculum initiative is a paradox. It represents both the last of a former age of curriculum initiatives and, I shall argue optimistically, the first of a new stock, at once both backward and forward looking in the way it is being implemented, and what it represents as a point of hope in a situation after the Education Reform Act, in which the responsibility has passed both to the school and to the national government at the apparent expense of the local education authority.

Let us consider first its origins. It depended in great measure on the leadership of one individual with at least one trusted senior partner and a growing following of others who were identified at different parts of the system by the leader or the senior partner, as people with three essential qualities – a shared perception of the vision, an empathy with the methods by which it could best be achieved and an ability to make things happen. In such a way can one identify Bill Walton, Roy Hedge and many others, some of whom are mentioned in or have contributed to this volume. I believe it impossible to overestimate the potency and vitality of that combination. Change, even within a complex organization such as an LEA, can happen in that way.

A microcosm, in the history of education since the war, one can see it at individual school level with the arrival or development of a headteacher. There are a legion of examples in primary schools especially in the old West Riding, in Leicestershire, Oxfordshire, Bristol, Shropshire, Cambridgeshire and the ILEA, where a headteacher has shown the way, enabling curriculum and organizational change to happen and securing the growth of teachers and an enhancement of the children's learning environment. It is less common in secondary schools at the whole school level, because the logistics of the organization and the essential feudalism, conservatism and the constraints of the external examination system, the isolation and the individualism of the teachers in separate classroom boxes, have made it more difficult. Indeed most examples are of new schools where the team leader hand-picked her staff. More frequently in secondary schools, the examples are of individual departments, for example in science, where the occasion of the Nuffield development or more recently, integrated and balanced science, has provided a vehicle to release the natural team building and inspiration of successful teachers. If the complexity of a secondary school stacks the odds heavily against the success of innovatory leadership, how much more complex is the LEA where there are long and in-efficient lines of communication and not a few powerful groups whose vested interests are served by the preservation of the status quo.

Even so, mention of some of those places where great primary schools were, and still are to be found, give a clue to the way in which LEAs have illustrated successful methods of change in the past. Sir Alec Clegg provided exceptional leadership: he too identified some like-minded people who can make things happen, Arthur Stone, Basil Rocke, Arthur Monck, and Diana Jordan. It is said that when his advisers could not agree about school design, he would summon a trusted headteacher to decide. Wilson in Shropshire was a similar if less celebrated spirit; Henry Morris and George Edwards in Cambridgeshire, Allan Chorlton and Edith Moorhouse in Oxfordshire, Stuart Mason, Len Sealey and Andrew Fairbairn in Leicestershire. In Mason's biography, Brian Simon spoke of Mason's achievements in Leicestershire in the following way:-

> These developments may today be seen as controversial, but there is no doubt of their impact at the time, nor of the exhilarating atmosphere within the schools which Mason engendered and maintained. This was enhanced by other enthusiasms of the director and of the often brilliant team of advisers he recruited.... resource based, individualised learning was encouraged with the provision of carefully planned resource centres, workshops, individual and group learning areas and so on. In a sense Leicestershire's education experienced a veritable renaissance during these years.

And in the foreword Andrew Fairbairn, his successor, ruminated on his predecessor's good fortune as follows:-

> He could always rely on an Education Committee who would read his memoranda and listen to arguments from their officers.

But concluded rather ruefully:-

> In later years however one could not be certain that this would
> be the case.

Indeed Brian Simon (1988) commented on the difficulties of today's
Chief Education Officers by saying:-

> In the harsher climate of today this period may seem like a
> golden age. Certainly it is unlikely that Chief Education
> Officers will in future be able to carve out the space needed to
> set their own individual marks on an area of such importance.
> The whole atmosphere and context are changed; new priorities,
> though sharply contested, have taken the place of the old. (In
> Jones, D. (Ed.) (1988) *The Art of Education*).

There are clues there to other essential impediments of LEA change but
also there is a tone which implies a growing complexity for Chief
Education Officer leadership, a complexity which is inimical to a repeat
of such developments. Sheffield's case however suggests otherwise, for
surely nothing could be more politicized than the 'people's republic of
South Yorkshire' which is how Sheffield is fondly regarded outside?
Yet in those circumstances and in an era of cutback and of teacher
dispute and against great odds, a similar grand design has begun to be
realized.

Peter Newsam, whose example in the case of Inner London's
primary schools in the 1970s in the wake of William Tyndale is another
example in yet more political and unpropitious circumstances, recently
analyzed some of Sir Alec Clegg's essential qualities.

What would the Sheffield reader with Bill Walton in their mind's
eye for comparison make of Newsam's description of Clegg showing 'a
consistent, respectful and understanding of the past', 'a creative anti-
bureaucratic spirit looking to see how to get round whatever it is that is
getting in the way', or coming back to the office excited after seeing the
Red House project and telling colleagues to stay away otherwise 'one of
you is bound to find they are breaking the law and believe you have to
stop them', or the self-criticism 'tell me six things wrong with this
outfit'? What too, of the compassion evident in the book written with
Barbara Megson of individual children in disadvantaged circumstances,
or the gift of explaining complex ideas simply or the humour.
The contemporary Sheffield audience would surely say the same of
Walton – even if they apparently would add a little 'moodiness'. Clegg
had that too.

Even so there is something more. Leaders of this sort have other essential attributes: they have an amazing capacity not merely to express the complex in simple terms but they also have the ability to hold mirrors to people's activity and to enable them to see not merely how things are, but how to find words to express how they might otherwise be – in short to provide a vision and to enable thousands of participants to share that vision and even to take a few short steps towards making it a reality. It is a task made the easier in education because teachers deal daily with treating children not as they are but as they might become; they trade in the future, their fuel is improvement. Without it children are not really taught.

The task which Sheffield set itself was at a time of unpropitious circumstances noted in the passages quoted from the Mason biography. The issue over which leadership was being exercised by Sheffield's Chief Education Officer was a very bold one at any time. He deployed the expedient of appealing direct to the teachers at the grass roots and to their headteachers. In essence he was essaying a transformation of the secondary experience.

What was different from all previous attempts was the bold and open declaration of intent of the vision. Most theorists – and I confess as a practitioner, instinctively I was inclined in similar circumstances so to behave – would say that to achieve success in a really grand enterprise it is unwise to declare the full picture for fear of frightening off the mountaineers from a climb too steep to contemplate. As an aside it might be argued that the government is in precisely such a position with the Education Reform Act: moreover they lack the lines of communication and natural common purpose established in the Sheffield Educational community. It says much for the timing, the sensitivity, the persistence and the judgment of the Sheffield initiative, that so much has been accomplished from so open a declaration of intent.

If leadership was one and perhaps the most important of the lessons to be drawn from the Sheffield experience, there are others worthy of note. One of the qualities needed to breathe reality into the vision is that of not allowing difficulties to get in your way, by being creative and unbureaucratic in a way which sometimes tests the bounds of propriety. Sheffield turned its attention to the imaginative use of secondments because it could see that it needed to ensure that there was creative time for teachers so their imagination might be unlocked. Indeed it was an authority that recognized the four needs of teachers. (One may regret in parenthesis that they are needs rather than rights, since the education scene throughout the country would be better if every teacher had the opportunity to have his/her energies released.) The four needs are: respect and recognition, permitting circumstances, responsibility and new experience. Walton's respect for teachers is evident in the letters sent to schools, in the talks given within and outside Sheffield: in consequence, the education service from the top seems to identify with the classroom teacher, even the child, in that teacher's classroom. In the Sheffield development teachers were clear of their responsibilities too, and they were given not merely time but encouraged to take risks and to innovate with a formative evaluator and tutor alongside, acting almost as coaches and partners in the enterprise. Above all Sheffield saw the need for time for teachers: so they examined the possibilities of the imaginative use of the untapped pool for seconded teachers in order that the most might be made of any new experiences offered to teachers outside the classroom.

An examination of the Chartered Institute of Public Finance and Accountancies (CIPFA) annual education estimates, from the late 1970s to the mid 1980s provides the clues to those local education authorities which, usually through the shrewdness of their Chief Education Officers and with the co-operation of the County Treasurers, had found the key to unlock hidden resources to facilitate school change and development. The figures of teachers on secondment appear for the first time in the CIPFA estimates of 1978/1979. Sheffield at that time seconded six primary and eleven secondary teachers: along with those of other LEAs it was probably an inherited pattern of secondments, the use of which was not important if budgets were buoyant. After the oil crisis, local government finances took on an increasingly bedraggled appearance as central government squeezed their contribution to the rate support grant and cut back public expenditure: the mysteries of distribution meant that the effects on the education service were felt randomly across the country, affected in no small measure by the particular political complexion of the LEA – the Conservative counties in the main responding more promptly – and by the strength of the education lobby. Naturally those wishing to find ways of protecting or even embellishing their school provision, cast around to find ingenious methods of finance. A few eyes fell on the untapped pool for the cost of seconding teachers to approved long courses at universities, polytechnics and colleges of education. It was natural that they should do so. After all, the expansion of the polytechnics had been enabled by the pooling of expenditure. As consensus broke down about acceptable local government behaviour and playing by the rules, so some poly- technics flourished as their particular LEA argued that to increase the polytechnics' expenditure at less than the real cost was a worthwhile good: and as it was a shared expenditure among all LEAs whether they provided a polytechnic or not, and based entirely on the number of secondary school pupils in a particular LEA, it cost them very little. The arrangements encouraged power without responsibility and provided a major loophole in plans to curb local expenditure; for the individual LEA it was unimportant, collectively it was serious. Not surprisingly the government eventually stopped it.

Similar considerations clearly applied to the much smaller pool for teachers seconded to attend long courses. As some LEAs realized nobody had noticed that pool. Why should they, when only 1,367 teachers from a teaching force of 447,000 teachers were expected to be on such courses in 1978/79?

Moreover the rules governing the pool at first sight discouraged those inclined to use it. After all, so the story went, the LEA had to shoulder the cost of 25 per cent of the seconded teachers' salaries and the whole cost of their replacement. Of course this was true but as my own County Treasurer was eventually persuaded, that meant that the LEA actually made money on the transaction if it happened to be the case that the particular teachers seconded were more senior post holders – a factor encouraged by rules which prohibited the second- ment of anyone in their first five years of teaching.

Suddenly the hard pressed LEA would be persuaded that the way to cope with falling rolls and an over-supply of teachers was not to confine their tactics to redundancy or early retirement schemes but to promote massive programmes of inservice training, both to promote intellectual debate and curriculum development and to save money. Like the other pool however, one LEA's excesses were paid for by the rest since the money was pooled among LEAs. So long as only a few indulged in excesses the pool was safe, and as has been noted, the apparent disincentive to the superficially inclined was the 25 per cent cost of the seconded teacher.

It is worth adding that it is a matter of national regret now that more did not take advantage of the scheme and that the pool was capped and replaced by a centrally controlled specific grant in 1987/8: had it not been, there would have been fewer early retirements which now add up to a huge problem of teacher supply.

A study of the CIPFA annual estimates 1978/9–1985/6 reveals those LEAs who were alive to the potential of the pool. Among the first were Leeds, Northamptonshire and Oxfordshire. Leeds, it may be surmized from the statistics, shared their secret with the West Yorkshire Metropolitan districts, all of whom seemed in that period, at least from the evidence of the CIPFA returns, to increase their secondments.

Initially Sheffield was not one of those authorities. In the last week of September 1985, however, Bill Walton went to Stockholm where he and I met for the first time and had the mutual misfortune to share a fairly cramped bedroom which overlooked a busy and noisy street: moreover their local disco appeared to be located in the room immediately below. There was in consequence much opportunity for discussion about the role and practice of Education Officers. I freely confess that it was the best piece of inservice training I ever engineered for myself, as we exchanged notes eagerly about the longer term purposes, principles and everyday practices, devices and problems of a county and a Metropolitan LEA. I learned much of subsequent value to Oxfordshire. We debated at some length the pool of teacher secondments. I think that helped Sheffield.

The Sheffield scheme for school focused secondments and curriculum initiative relied on a partnership between the LEA, the University and the Polytechnic: that it had fewer flaws in its implementation must, in some small measure, be due to the Stockholm conversation since I was certainly able to amuse Bill Walton with tales of the unexpected.

The key feature, of course, for a large programme has to be a close collaboration with local providers, since very few teachers with more than five years' teaching experience, and usually with family commitments are likely to want to go to a different part of the country to study. Making the best of that precondition, however, is another matter. First it is clear that the University and/or Polytechnic should have been very interested in such a large increase in students, not least because of the massive fee income it represented. Indeed the occasion for negotiation with such institutions, which might not normally see themselves as mainly concerned with mainstream provision of education in an area, had the potential to bring unintended side benefits. It certainly did in Oxford where other departments of the Polytechnic began to expend energy to support the schooling system: within the University too, a network of dons was established to provide enrichment courses, seminars and workshops, both for individual schools and networks of schools in general. In the end the 'internship scheme' for teacher training also emerged and the first 'record of achievement' of what turned out to be a national venture in both spheres.

More important was for the LEA to bring a coherent strategy to this huge programme of secondment. They could be taken by individual teachers for lengths which were governed simply by the criteria for the approved course: a year or one term was the rule and it was only towards the end of the period of the pool that twenty-five day courses, providing welcome flexibility, became possible.

It remains my belief that only half-a-dozen LEAs thought strategically as opposed to tactically about the use of the pool. The tacticians simply saw the pool as a device – a means of saving money and managing falling rolls, through pushing away the oversupply of teachers for a year. It had the potential for something much more. The strategists thought of the possibilities of secondment for curriculum development and transforming the organization of schools.

In using secondments there were three possible models. The need of the individual for further training, retraining or refreshment, could often be made to coincide with the matter of falling rolls. The limitation of such an arrangement was that the return of the teacher to the school had very little impact on its collective purpose. Time and again the teacher was resocialized within the staff room or else left for promotion. Until very recently schools lacked any coherent staff development plan, for so many schools secondment time was such a rare event, indeed a luxury: very few schools so arranged their staffing resource that more than one member of the school might have time for visits and study. Of course with the advent of professional development days as a result of the Pay and Conditions Act, 1987, under the arrangements for the centrally controlled Government grant (GRIST/LEATGS) which replaced the secondments, all schools will now have professional development plans – with predictable benefits for school effectiveness.

The second model of secondment required discussion with a polytechnic or university in order to arrange the co-ordination of three or four secondments from the same school to look at the same issue which the school or the LEA might have identified as worthwhile. Instead of the isolate returning to be overwhelmed by the status quo of the majority of the staff, it held the promise, especially if a sufficient proportion of the staff were involved, of enabling a significant development of school thinking. The third model required an education authority to identify a group of individuals, not known to each other but sharing similar interests, from each of a number of schools, so that enthusiasts for that particular issue, drawn together, might gain impetus for LEA-wide change based on their work.

It seems that Sheffield saw all those possibilities clearly when they embarked on the school focused inservice scheme: in the main the project represents a combination of the second and third variants, i.e. LEA-wide but also intended to give the impetus to indepth change in the curriculum in a particular school.

Something peculiar to Sheffield was the emergence of a tutorial support team, a kind of alternative advisory force drawn from different agencies, e.g. seconded from the University to provide a potent, trustworthy, critical friend for the teachers and schools.

Such a clear lead and sense of direction is probably the easier to achieve at metropolitan district, than in a county where the communication lines are longer and a sense of identity less pronounced. A city such as Sheffield also has advantages of shared interest, hemmed in as it is by hills, with an intense history and a population the majority of whom had similar involvement in a few major industries. Steel was never far away from Sheffield's interests until its dramatic decline and the rapid growth of unemployment in the early 1980s. A shared sense of adversity not to say injustice may have been an subliminal factor conducive to change. After all when Sheffield floated its massive curriculum change affecting mainly secondary schooling, the school-teacher and parental rhetoric that success in schooling led to employment was demonstrably untrue. When that is so, the education of 14 and 15 year olds in particular reveals the uneasy peace for turbulent teenagers in compulsory schooling.

It is interesting to note that in its early days the massive second-ment programme ran into some of the same sort of difficulties which Oxfordshire experienced in close collaboration with the university and a polytechnic. There was the problem of persuading academics that the integrity of their award was of secondary importance as far as the school and the LEA was concerned. Requirements relating to written essays and examinations had to be adjusted. Moreover the volume of teachers embarking on the university end of the course produced pressures which tested the organizational qualities of the institution. It was not uncommon to hear complaints about the quality and relevance, sometimes even the organization of the university part of the experience. Sometimes the university was unjustly blamed for LEA failings. It was not surprising that it had to be changed as it developed. There were, too, among the seconded a fair number of cynics who were only too ready to exploit any inefficiency, either for the purpose of argument, or to undermine its purpose.

It has to be stressed however, that the logistical problems pale into insignificance beside the two great benefits which the scheme brought to Sheffield (and which I believe were also experienced in Oxfordshire over a longer period more gradually). First there was an almost tangible increase in the intellectual curiosity and debate among teachers on a wide scale. Without it of course there is not much respect for that sense of lively enquiry which causes teachers to search 'every-which-way' to find the key to unlock the minds of each and every one of their pupils. It resides imperishable in many teachers. The Sheffield scheme ignited it in many a teacher who might otherwise not have had the time or space to think beyond the daily crisis of classroom and school. There was a substantial increase in teacher morale – another vital prerequisite to an improvement in children's learning.

There are other features of the Sheffield scheme which appear capable of generalization. One deserves the closest study. Sheffield initially resorted to agencies other than the advisory service or inspectorate to implement wholesale change – at the very least, and as I have already noted, they set up an alternative – the tutorial support team, who developed a consultancy role – to provide the trust and courage to the pioneers in the schools. Indeed it is possible to read between the lines that there was a lack of empathy, even, in some quarters, opposition to the changes being advocated. In a sense an advisory service becomes the defender of the status quo. Most advisers have risen through the ranks of the teaching profession and have an uneasy relationship with headteachers who occupy a rank many of them never reach. Typically it is from the ranks of deputy headteachers and heads of departments that the advisers and inspectors are recruited to local authorities. They then suffer from the disadvantage of seeing only a part of the educational scene. To headteachers they seem not as credible as Education Officers who, although from similar backgrounds, have to combine in their everyday business, the giving of advice with the reality of management and of the limitations of resources and who, more over see the whole of the scene over which they preside.

Individual advisers, especially those with headteacher backgrounds, although sometimes those others with incisive, boundless and cheerful enthusiasms, transcend such criticisms. It is an elusive issue – the more urgent to solve in the light of the changes in the 1988 Education Reform Act which may encourage the unwary LEA to hard models of inspection. 'Unwary' because the 'hard-done-by' schools will have recourse to grant-maintained status in which case they can buy their own advice and inspection on their terms. Perhaps that provides a clue to effective support work whether by advisers, inspectors or, as in the Sheffield case, tutor teams – it works best where there is a contract on the school's terms. Less unproductive time is taken up in subsequent defensive recrimination.

Two other factors in the Sheffield experience deserve notice. The first is in the variety of initiatives most of which, (although much less remarked, but as real as the attention to primary practice especially in the early years), have a common ingredient of the grand design to change in the secondary curriculum. The TVEI project and the lower attainers' scheme were already off the ground, but the school focused secondments, the Sheffield curriculum, and more recently the records of achievement movement and the 'Compact' were all set in train with the express purpose of securing purchase on change in the second curriculum and school organization. More recently the Chief Education Officer's letters have pointed to the common theme.

The second feature is however unique to Sheffield. It is the bold declaration of intent and the sudden intensive effort at change which has been noted before. It is remarkable that so much has been achieved in so short a time. To the cynic it will appear at first that there is little progress but in a sense the secondary schools in Sheffield will never be quite the same again. I remember visiting the city on 18 December 1987, to spend a day briefly meeting some of those closely engaged in the process of visiting schools. At Brian Wilcox's invitation I responded at the end of a hectic tour to the request to provide some sort of superficial evaluative feedback. I did so in the following letter:-

> Of course it's always dangerous to give a snap feedback ... especially if you are dictating it while driving down the M1 on the Friday before Christmas week! (The latter will, I hope, excuse some incoherence in what follows.)
>
> But you did ask for impressions ... so here they are.
>
> First I was very impressed by the energy, enthusiasm and *shared* commitment and purpose of those I met. I was also struck by their ability. Moreover, I did have a chance to wander randomly in Newfield and City School, and certainly in the latter encountered one who clearly was by nature inclined to be critical. So I think I did see some bits of a rounded picture. The shared commitment and purpose however was unusual and,

from my point of view, enviable. In a way it represented something I've been striving to achieve in Oxfordshire: it was as though I suddenly saw in reality what I believe is just round the corner here. Of course you can discount for it being a one-day visit and seeing only a little.

Second and connected, that shared commitment seemed to have been achieved by an approach to the process of change which is unusual. In a curious way the initiative is top-down (letter of December 1985) without being top-down. Did the letter perhaps simply give voice to something everyone (well, a lot anyway) were thinking about secondary schools? I always think with secondary school curriculum and particularly the organization of the school we all are like Copernicus but continue to behave as if we really will fall off the edge of the world if we *act* on the Copernican theory. There were really hopeful signs, I thought, especially in the expressed views of the Heads, senior staff and teachers in the schools that progress was at last being made. The voyage, as it were, had started. Half the crew, of course, will be shouting that the boat *will* fall off the edge of the world and quite a few who keep chanting 'Copernicus' at the top of their voices are doubtless doing so to keep their spirits up.

That was where I was impressed by the support staff and the little fleet of supply ships at SFD CAR and in the invaluable centre at Broomgrove Road. That model of development seems to me pure gold and will need to be sustained at all cost. Otherwise – pushing the seagoing Copernican analogy to destruction (if it's not already) – the crew on the main ship will claim that they are running out of food, say they know the world is really round but suggest that they'll have to go back to port for more fuel. With budget cuts looming that would be even more of a temptation. I should guess, incidentally, you'll find the interface of the tutor support from Broomgrove Road with the role of the General Adviser for the school, an issue needing some attention once it's in place if tension is to be creative and not disruptive. A detail, but I like the way you are using the evaluator as a facilitator and historian as well ... or that's how it appeared to me.

I think, too, you'd need a major initiative, probably through the development of the record of achievement end of things, in making sure the partnership with parents and their expectations are changed, lifted and improved. We started a modest parental newsletter. ... I expect you've done a lot and I forgot to ask Roy and Bill, so forgive me if I'm teaching grandmother.

So I was left hoping...

that TVEI extension would allow a final bringing together of CDI, TVEI, SFD, etc.,
that in three years' time you could let schools use devolved funds to devise their own corporate staff development plan with INSET money, but not before,
that the way you present exam. results would reflect the changed value systems being tackled in your schools,
that you personally would do another seminal book on curriculum analysis, reflecting the changed basis of the secondary curriculum now the sailors are voyaging on a different compass,
that with your perceptive eyes you will find the ways of expressing the everyday organization features of the school in Copernican rather than Ptolemaic terms.
Well, you did ask ... and the journey down the M1 is a long one. Above all I pray that all of you in Sheffield get the luck you deserve. It's important for the rest of us that you do. I wish you were closer to us.
Am copying this to Roy Hedge, Bill Walton and John Roberts and apologise for its length, incoherence and presumption.

So what we have seen is a lesson in leadership with a clear purpose and an eviable ability to relate to key managers and teachers in the whole of the city's education service, in the imaginative use of secondments linked to a university and a polytechnic, in the co-ordination of various initiatives, and the relative lack of involvement of an advisory service in the name of a curriculum change which was the logical outcome of various changes in education and society but finding expression in a bold departure from the past and the reinforcement such a legacy has received from the 1988 Act.

The assessment must be that it is one of very few such ventures in the history of local education authorities. Although comparable to anything attempted before in the matter of qualitative as opposed to quantitative improvement, its scale and speed is probably unrivalled. Elsewhere commentators have suggested that the use of language – 'ownership, partnership' feature strongly – indeed is a key feature in the shared sense of urgency and success; sufficient perhaps to carry the venturers through the inevitable difficulties and tribulations. Certainly that is a telling feature too in the process of change: it can be traced in the language of the West Riding and of rural Oxfordshire in the 1950s and '60s in the pioneering work of primary schools, and it is of course a feature of curriculum development elsewhere.

There are two further questions posed by the Sheffield Development which need to be addressed. Will the Sheffield Development now founder in the face of apparently contradictory forces at a national level? Would such a scheme be possible again given the changes implied in the Education Reform Act? Most commentators think it unlikely. Indeed the Education Reform Act removes the power from local education authorities and redistributes it either to the school or to central government and in some instances, confusingly to both. At first sight that is bad news for LEAs; Sir David Eccles' 'Secret Garden' of the curriculum is now public property. Moreover, there is little room for doubt in curriculum matters: the first parliamentary orders for science and mathematics made chilling reading. Stripped of the friendly, colourful and glossy presentation in the reports from working groups chaired by Jeff Thompson and Duncan Graham, they appeared to be what they are – a prescribed and fairly detailed, if slightly impractical and at some stages absurd and inappropriate not to say over-ambitious set of syllabus guidelines dressed up as programmes of study. The attainment targets of particular levels will force the less confident teacher to concentrate on ensuring that the implied information is well understood by pupils at particular stages: it will be only natural for the teachers to feel that they could sleep the easier if their pupils really understand the particular ground implied by the programmes of study. Already those who recently introduced a modification of Nuffield to the age range 11–13 are talking of substantial changes in what they do. Moreover well meaning local inspectorates and advisory services using bespoke LEATGSs (Central Inservice) money and Education Support Grants will hold the hands of the less confident teachers so that they might better understand what is expected of them. The steamroller of the National Curriculum Council and the power over external examination qualification held by the Schools Examination and Assessment Council will together for a while constitute a powerful force which will lead to a narrowing of possibility. After all that is what focusing does: it narrows as well as sharpens one's field of vision.

Consider the words of Bill Walton's original letter '... curriculum domains need to be inter-related ... assessment and monitoring can no longer be sub-contracted to an examination system immersed in the "cult of the fact"'. It has to be acknowledged that at first blush the national imperative is unsympathetic to such ideas. Yet one cannot help noticing the determined way in which the initiative has been kept in play despite the enormous budgetary problems facing the Sheffield Authority: moreover there is sufficient evidence in the scheme to suggest that schools themselves now feel they 'own' the idea and will find ways to keep it alive as power is passed to them. Two of those ways probably lie in the contextualization both of the youngsters' assessments within the record of achievement and of the school's performance in whatever collective record of achievement is presented to the community. The former is particularly important for the primary school where teachers who hitherto have been used to construing the development of the whole child across the whole curriculum, may be thrown off balance by the urgent insistence on a discrete approach both by inservice training and by receipt of information from the separate subject reports and orders (science, mathematics, English, technology, etc.). As for the school report, the importance of the presentation cannot be over-emphasized given the pressures of destructive competition between schools implied by the market forces now released by the Education Reform Act.

On both these issues moreover, there are signs that Sheffield is alive to the problem: Sheffield's record of achievement *is* intended for the whole 5–16 age range and Sheffield is one of the authorities investigating performance indicators and school effectiveness with a network of other interested parties elsewhere in the country. It seems unlikely, therefore, that the National Curriculum and the Education Reform Act will mean much more to Sheffield than some interesting white water does to the successful canoeist.

The wider question, namely the impact of the Education Reform Act and the possibility of similar future reforms elsewhere is in some ways the more interesting. The removal of powers to government and to schools *seems* to emasculate LEAs. In a sense, however, other LEAs have achieved things by a longer term influence. LEAs in future will have to achieve *change by influence*, by giving a lead and by making resources available to support the change. In the latter respect the 7 per cent – 10 per cent element of the budget held naturally under LMS is directly analogous to the ESGs held by central government. Indeed, precisely that illustration is used by government explanations of the scheme. In short, LEAs which eschew over-direction and avoid the siren sounds of inspection and monitoring may well find themselves able to promote more rather than less change in the future. LEAs will have a life in their present form for at least five years as they are needed to implement the change already in train as a result of the Education Reform Act. It will be possible for the determined to turn that change to their own agenda. There is at least one rule about legislation, namely that it never turns out as parliament intends. Already the curriculum reformers are talking of the imaginative repackaging of the attainment targets in different subject groupings – what Walton would call 'across the domains'. Even as I write, those planning the NCC Curriculum INSET contract are gathering in hotels where the best and most progressive of practitioners are devising the keys to unlock the shackles of the National Curriculum. After all, thoughtful teachers can handle even the potentially most arid of materials.

So where and when will the next change occur? The ingredients I submit will be the same as those of the Sheffield initiative, namely strong, sympathetic leadership, time for teachers to work collectively for curriculum change and people within the system who are unbureaucratic. Much will happen at the level of the department and of the school. It will be for the LEA to foster it, make it interdependent, legitimize it, set a climate in which the free spirits can flourish. Generations ahead will look to the Sheffield initiative, not as the end of one era but as the forerunner of a new.

Endpiece: Evaluation

Kath Aspinwall, Elizabeth Clough and Bob Gibbs

This book has set out to offer a series of perspectives on different aspects, processes, principles of SCI rather than a summative evaluation of the initiative. However, the project has been the subject of considerable evaluation activity from the outset and the account would not be complete without some reference to this work. The LEA has employed one person to spend a full year evaluating the first year of SFS/D and subsequently to extend this work to other aspects of SCI as part of a wider GRIST evaluation brief. A second evaluator has been involved with the TVEI Pilot and the CDI (or LAPP) Project. The advisory team has also contributed to this process and five teachers (including three heads) were seconded on the One Term Training Opportunity, OTTO, programme to undertake further work in this area. Throughout the three years of the initiative, in–school evaluation has formed all or part of the commission of individual secondees, the issue has been addressed in the supporting programmes and is very much part of the agenda more generally within the LEA.

A variety of people within schools and the LEA have been interviewed at different time and about different aspects of the initiative. Pupils and a smaller number of parents have also been interviewed, classrooms, meetings, parts of the programmes have been observed, questionnaires circulated. The evidence from these sources has informed much of the writing in this book. The initiative is difficult to assess on any objectives led criteria, except on an individual commission basis, because of its open ended nature and much of the evaluation that has been undertaken has been of a qualitative, illuminative nature. However, it is possible to point to some generalizable conclusions with the following factors receiving almost universal acceptance within the LEA:-

a.   The is a more effective use of secondment than in the past, both

in terms of the effect on schools and the personal and professional development of teachers.

b. Teacher morale, in particular that of secondees, has been raised.

c. There are visible effects in all schools on the curriculum,
teaching styles and organization, although amounts vary considerably.

d. The discussion that has been engendered amongst staff is
leading to the development of new levels of understanding of
curriculum issues.

e. The sharing of ideas between schools and across pyramids/
clusters has encouraged the formation of useful links.

Effects on Secondees

Almost all secondees have found the experience to have been a positive
one, even in situations where they have felt some disappointment or
reservation about the long term effect of their work. These claims are
substantiated by their heads and co-ordinators and include:-

(i)   Personal development, this usually refers to matters such as
increased confidence and the realization of the effects of their
behaviour on colleagues and pupils.

(ii) Professional development, in the form of increased understanding of both their own and other curriculum areas, and of
the ways schools are, or might be, organized and managed.

(iii) The development of new skills in working with other staff
which is proving helpful on 'Curriculum Days' and in staff
meetings.

(iv) Renewed energy and enthusiasm, 'revitalization'. In a few
cases both secondees and others felt this had been overdone,
proving somewhat of a trial to other staff.

(v)   Many secondees report feeling 'privileged' and frequently
suggest that such an experience should be the entitlement of
all teachers over time.

It is inevitable that some secondees and commissions haved proved to
be more effective than others and from the accumulated evidence it has
been possible to identify factors that contribute to successful outcomes.
The choice of secondee and the ways in which they were chosen, their
commissions agreed and how other staff continue to be involved are all

crucial factors. Where staff feel that particular people or activities have been imposed upon them there is little chance of their whole-hearted support, although some secondees have overcome the inadequacy of a selection process by the quality of their work. The influence of the head and senior management is also significant. Visible, but sensitive, support is essential and the movement away from a reliance on hierarchy does not prevent lack of support from the top demoralizing those involved in any development. The general climate within a school has an effect on what is possible. An awareness that all of those in an organization bear some responsibility for the quality of relationships within it is a helpful factor, as is a recognition that support is necessary for those involved in innovation. Lastly, the pace at which matters proceed has considerable effect on what happens and on the individuals concerned. It is essential to review this regularly in order to maintain the impetus whilst avoiding innovation fatigue.

The quantity and variety of evaluation studies that have been carried out have led to a good deal of reflection on the purpose of such activities. Whilst there is a place for a 'history' of an innovation and occasional summative documents, there is a more urgent need for information that can be available quickly enough to influence ongoing practice. Actual involvement in the evaluation process is clearly linked to commitment to take appropriate action. There is growing interest in rendering more systematic and available to others the kinds of reflection and review that occur continuously in schools, with a much more selective use of any in depth 'research' studies. Evaluation activities must support and refine practice not become a preoccupation that diverts energy in a way that distorts or confuses. A clearly articulated policy towards review and evaluation and a shared commitment to respond to any insights or findings in all institutions and at all levels within the initiative must play a central part within SCI or any such development. The evaluation activities that have taken place have encouraged not only reconsideration of the developing practice but also a rethinking of the evaluation process itself.

A Selection of SCI Evaluation Reports

ANWYLL, S. (1988) *Primary SFS: Back in School*, (mimeo) Sheffield LEA.
ASPINWALL, K. (1986) *'SFS: An Idea that has Found its Time' – Some Initial Response to Sheffield's School Focused Secondment Programme*, (mimeo) Sheffield LEA.

ASPINWALL, K. (1986) *Advisory Team Reports on the SFS Programme: Summary No 1* (mimeo) Sheffield LEA.

ASPINWALL, K. (1987) *Advisory Team Reports on the SFS Programme: Summary No 2.* (mimeo) Sheffield LEA.

ASPINWALL, K. (1987) *Insider Evaluator.* Paper at BERA annual conference, Manchester (mimeo)

ASPINWALL, K. (1987) *Interviews with Secondees: Report No 1. The Process of Selection.* (mimeo) Sheffield LEA.

ASPINWALL, K. (1987) *Interviews with Secondees: Report No 2. Attitudes and Aspirations* (mimeo) Sheffield LEA.

ASPINWALL, K. (1987) *A climate for Change: A Report on the First Year of Sheffield's School Focused Secondment Initiative* (mimeo) Sheffield LEA.

ASPINWALL, K. (1988) *Curriculum Change Across Schools* Paper given at BEMAS conference, (mimeo) Cardiff.

ASPINWALL, K. (1988) *Curriculum Development Initiatives: Some Factors Influencing Successful Outcomes,* (mimeo) Sheffield LEA.

ASPINWALL, K. (1988) *'Uncompleted Business': Interviews with Secondees, Report No 3* (mimeo) Sheffield LEA.

ASPINWALL, K. (1988) SFS/SFD. *'I Learn Best When....': Emerging Changes in Classroom Experience* (mimeo) Sheffield LEA.

ASPINWALL, K. (1988) *Perceptions of SFS December 1988.* (mimeo) Sheffield LEA.

ASPINWALL, K. (1989) 'A bit of the sun': "Teacher development through an LEA initiative", in WOODS, P. (Ed.) *Working for Teacher Development,* Peter Francis: Dereham, Norfolk,. pp. 118–135.

ASPINWALL, K. and GRANT, R. (1988) *Primary school focused Development 1987–8* (mimeo) Sheffield LEA.

ASPINWALL, K. and NIXON, J. (1986) *Managing change: A team approach* (mimeo) Sheffield LEA.

ASPINWALL, K. and NIXON, J. (1987) *Report on the Conference 'The Coordination of School Focused Secondment' for in-school coordinators* (mimeo) Sheffield LEA.

FULKER, P., REGAN, P. and THOMPSON, J. (1987) *The Sheffield SFS Programme, an Evaluation: Management Implications for Schools and LEAs* (mimeo) Sheffield LEA.

GARFORTH, J. (1988) *Evaluation of the Sheffield Curriculum Initiative in Secondary Schools* (mimeo) Sheffield LEA.

NIXON, J. (1986) *Feeling the Change: Thoughts on the Evaluation Task for Sheffield* Division of Education, University of Sheffield.

NIXON, J. (Ed.) (1987) *Curriculum Change: The Sheffield Experience* (USDE Papers in Education) Division of Education, Sheffield University.

NIXON, J. (1987) *Sheffield TVEI: Industry, Parents and the Changing Curriculum* (An Interim Evaluation Report) Division of Education, University of Sheffield.

NIXON, J. (1987) *The Time of the Tortoise: Curriculum Development in Context* (Sheffield LAPP, Evaluation Paper No 1) Division of Education, Sheffield University.

NIXON, J. (1987) *The Management of Long Term Change through a Medium-Term*

Project: Curriculum Development in Action (Sheffield LAPP, Evaluation Paper No 2) Division of Education, Sheffield University.

NIXON, J. (1988) *Sheffield TVEI: Transition and Continuity* (Final Evaluation Report) Division of Education, Sheffield University.

NIXON, J. (1988) 'The Management of Long Term Change through a Fixed Term Project' *Curriculum* 9–2 pp. 65–68.

POLLARD, K. (1987) *The Management of New Teaching Learning Styles in Secondary Schools* (mimeo) Sheffield: Department of Educational Management, Sheffield City Polytechnic.

THRELFALL, P. (1986) *Sheffield School Focused Secondment Scheme. A Personal View* (mimeo) Sheffield; Department of Educational Management, Sheffield City Polytechnic.

SKELTON, A. (1989) *Lower School Curriculum Development in Sheffield: An Interim Report* (CDI) Division of Education, Sheffield University.

(Evaluation reports from individual schools have not been included).

Notes on Contributors

Elizabeth Clough is a tutor on the Sheffield School Focused Development Programme. She has taught in secondary schools and higher education, and has a particular research interest in the field of children's learning and its assessment.

Bill Walton is Chief Education Officer of Sheffield LEA and is currently President of the Society of Education Officers 1989–90. He entered LEA administration after experience in schools and industry.

Roy Hedge is the Director of the School Focused Development Programme and the Curriculum and Assessment Resource. He has taught in schools, colleges and universities in England and New York.

Rosie Grant has tutored the primary teachers on the SFD programme since 1985. Previously she taught in primary schools and has researched into primary classroom practices, women teacher's careers and evaluated LEA projects.

Kath Aspinwall is currently employed as the LEATG evaluator for Sheffield LEA. Prior to this she was an advisory teacher and has taught in nursery, primary, further and higher education.

Douglas Finlayson, formerly of the University of Liverpool, is an independent development consultant who works with individuals, groups, and organizations. He has been associated with SCI since 1985.

Carole Goodwin is a tutor on the Sheffield School Focused Development programme. She has taught in community schools in Leicestershire, researched into education for physically handicapped children and was an educational psychologist for ten years.

Daryl Agnew is an advisory teacher for equal opportunities (gender) and has tutored on the SFD programme. She has taught English and drama in secondary schools and co-ordinated the Equal Opportunities/Sheffield LEA Careers Intervention Project 1983/84.

Jeanie Hedge has been a tutor at the Curriculum and Assessment Resource for two years, promoting recording achievement and experience. She has taught English, PSE and Careers in a wide variety of schools including primary, secondary and special.

Colin Martin has been a tutor at the Curriculum and Assessment Resource for two years, promoting recording achievement and experience. Prior to this he taught in comprehensive schools and was head of biology and a year head.

Pat McAteer is a teacher at Notre Dame school, Sheffield. She was seconded to the SFD programme in 1987/88.

Linda Power is a teacher at Prince Edward Nursery, First and Middle school. She was seconded to the SFD programme in 1987/88.

Ian Anniss is a tutor on the SFD programme. Prior to this he was involved in a research project on Post Primary Reorganization for Sheffield LEA. He has taught in secondary schools and higher education.

Bob Gibbs is a tutor on the SFD programme. He has taught in primary, middle and secondary schools, and for LEAs as SCIP co-ordinator and TRIST adviser. His current interests include the role of consultancy in educational development and change.

Bob Driskell is headteacher of Sir Harold Jackson school.

Graham Evans is headteacher at Herries secondary school.

Jenny Frankish, formerly headteacher at Gleadless Valley secondary school, is now assistant principal of Parkwood tertiary college.

Keith Pollard is headteacher of Handsworth Grange secondary school.

Charles Sisum is headteacher of Wisewood secondary school.

Peter Clough worked for some ten years in secondary and special schools before moving to Sheffield University Division of Education as course tutor for the special needs programme and co-director of the special needs evaluation and research group.

Fritz Bohnsack is Professor of Education at the University of Essen in West Germany. He was visiting professor at the Division of Education of the University of Sheffield from August 1988 to February 1989. His present main interest are school focused and school based in-service training of teachers.

Tim Brighouse, currently Professor of Education at Keele University, was Chief Education Officer in Oxfordshire for more than a decade, Deputy Education Officer in ILEA and worked in administration and teaching in various English and Welsh schools. He has contributed extensively to educational debate, through writing books, articles and speaking at conferences and teacher workshops.

Glossary

ASP	Advanced Studies Programme
BTEC	Business and Technician Education Council
CAR	Curriculum and Assessment Resource
CDI	Curriculum Development Initiative
CEO	Chief Education Officer
CIPFA	Chartered Institute of Public Finances and Accountancies
CPVE	Certificate of Pre-Vocational Education
CSE	Certificate of Secondary Education
CSG	Commission Support Group
DES	Department of Education and Science
ERA	Education Reform Act (1988)
ESG	Education Support Grant
FE	Further Education
GCSE	General Certificate of Secondary Education
GRIDS	Guidelines for Review and Internal Development in Schools
GRIST	Grant-Related In-Service Training
HE	Higher Education
HMI	Her Majesty's Inspectorate
ILEA	Inner London Education Authority
INSET	In-Service Education and Training
ISATT	International Study Association on Teacher Thinking
LAPP	Lower Attaining Pupils Programme
LEA	Local Education Authority
LEATGS	LEA Training Grant Scheme
LFM	Local Financial Management
LMS	Local Management of Schools
NFER	National Foundation for Education Research
MSC	Manpower Services Commission
MST	Management Support Team
NCC	National Curriculum Council
OTTO	One Term Training Opportunity

PRAISE   Pilot Record of Achievement in Schools Evaluation
PTA   Parent-Teachers Association
RAE   Record of Achievement and Experience
RANSC   Record of Achievement National Steering Committee
SAT   Standardized Assessment Task
SBI   School-Based Inset
SCDC   Schools Curriculum Development Committee
SCI   Sheffield Curriculum Initiative
SCIP   School Curriculum Industry Partnership
SEAC   Secondary Examinations and Assessment Council
SEBP   Sheffield Education Business Partnership
SEC   Secondary Examination Council
SFD   School Focused Development
SFS   School Focused Secondment
SUMES   Sheffield Unified Multicultural Education Service
TA   Training Agency
TRIST   TVEI-Related In-Service Training
TVEI   Technical and Vocational Education Initiative
TVEI-E   Technical and Vocational Education Initiative Extension
UDE   University Department of Education
YTS   Youth Training Scheme

Index